SAIL TALL SHIPS!

A DIRECTORY OF SAIL TRAINING AND ADVENTURE AT SEA

EDITED BY:
LINCOLN P. PAINE

NINTH EDITION

THE AMERICAN SAIL TRAINING ASSOCIATION
NEWPORT, RHODE ISLAND

Published by:

American Sail Training Association (ASTA®)
47 Bowen's Wharf
PO Box 1459
Newport, RI 02840

Phone: (401) 846-1775
Fax: (401) 849-5400

ISBN 0-9636483-2-2

Library of Congress Cataloguing-in-Publication Data

Sail Tall Ships! A Directory of Sail Training and Adventure at Sea
9th ed./edited by Lincoln P. Paine

American Sail Training Association

1996 Board of Directors

Bartlett S. Dunbar - Chairman
Richard Bailey - Vice Chair
Per H. M. Lofving - Vice Chair
Jeffrey N. Parker - Secretary
W. Bruce Quackenbush, Jr. - Treasurer
Pamela C. Wuerth - Executive Director

Alexander M. Agnew
W. Jeffrey Bolster
David C. Brink
Ned Chalker
Peter A. Evans
Robert C. Glover III
Thomas J. Gochberg
Pete Hall
Deborah R. Hayes
Terry G. Klaus
Carmel G. Locey
Joseph A. Maggio
Wilbert A. Pinkerton, Jr.
William D. Pinkney
Daniel P. Quinn
Michael J. Rauworth
Scott W. Raymond
Nancy H. Richardson
Walter Rybka
Gail R. Shawe
Sidney A. Thompson
Alix T. Thorne
Barclay H. Warburton IV
VADM Thomas R. Weschler USN (Ret)
John C. Wigglesworth
CAPT David V. V. Wood USCG (Ret)

Commodore's Council

Harry H. Anderson, Jr.
David C. Brink
Pete Hall
Nancy H. Richardson
Gail R. Shawe
VADM Thomas R. Weschler USN (Ret)
Pamela C. Wuerth

Supporting Members

Alexander & Alexander
Mr. Withers Davis

Barrett Companies
Mr. Thomas Barrett

Conventures, Inc.
Ms. Dusty S. Rhodes

Cutty Sark North America
Mr. Paul Bermudez

Hansen Marine Associates, Inc.
Mr. David B. Markell

International Special Risks, Inc.
Mr. David E. Sargent

Outfitters/USA
Ms. Karen Hanson

Scripps Howard, Inc.
Mr. Charles E. Scripps

Societé du Vieux-Port de Montréal
Msr. Sylvain DesChamps

WIMCO
Mr. Barclay H. Warburton IV

Mr. Peter A. Evans
Mr. Paul Gaston
Mr. Thomas J. Gochberg
Mr. and Mrs. Frederick Hood
Mr. Jerold T. Humphreys, Sr.
Captain Kelly Kellogg
Ms. Mari Oyanagi
Mr. Wilbert A. Pinkerton, Jr.
Mr. Michael J. Rauworth
Mr. David W. Ray
Mr. and Mrs. Joseph A. Ribaudo
Mr. Robert S. Scheu
Ms. Alix T. Thorne
Mr. John C. A. Watkins
CAPT Eric J. Williams III, USCG
Mr. John Thompson Woodhouse III

American Sail Training Association

Pamela C. Wuerth, Executive Director

With special thanks to: Alex Agnew, Richard Bailey, Beth Bonds, Ned Chalker, Bart Dunbar, Tom Gochberg, Halden Jensen, Carmel Locey, Michael Rauworth, Dusty Rhodes, Nancy Richardson, Walter Rybka, Gail Shawe, Alix Thorne, Barclay Warburton IV, John Wigglesworth, and David V. V. Wood.

Designed and Desktop Published by: Patricia Rae Linn

Cover photo by: Roger Archibald.

For interior photos designated as "ASTA file photos" we thank the photographers, especially Nancy Linden.

The ninth edition of the ASTA® *Sail Tall Ships! A Directory of Sail Training and Adventure at Sea* was desktop published on a Macintosh IIvc computer using MicrosoftWord, and QuarkXPress. Text is set in ITC-New Baskerville and Frugal Sans fonts.

The following registered marks are the property of the American Sail Training Association.

ASTA®
Tall Ships®
Tall Ships are Coming®
Return of the Tall Ships®
Tall Ships 2000®

Contents

"Whenever I find myself involuntarily passing before coffin warehouses, and bringing up the rear of every funeral I meet; and especially whenever my hypos get such an upper hand on me, that it requires a strong moral principle to prevent me from deliberately stepping into the street, and methodically knocking people's hats off — then, I account it high time to get to sea as soon as I can." — Herman Melville, *Moby Dick*

Roger Archibald photo

Foreword

In the United States and Canada, there are many sail training vessels which serve as laboratories and classrooms at sea. College and high school students regularly embark on semester-long voyages of offshore discovery while younger children explore local waters on grade-school field trips. Water, sediment and biological sampling provide students with tangible lessons in the marine environment as they themselves physically encounter the effect of wind and wave. Formal study aboard a ship is frequently referred to as sea education.

Historic vessels, or their reproductions, function as interpretive museum exhibits, conducting voyages of outreach to the public. Most North Americans can trace their ancestors' arrival by ship. The last sailing vessel to regularly carry immigrants to America still plies New England waters, now a sailing school vessel, extending her venerable history of more than one hundred years service — from fishing the Grand Banks to Arctic exploration to African packet.

There are reproductions and restorations of ships representative of each of America's naval conflicts. We may board important sailing ships of the American Revolution, the War of 1812, the Civil War and some which played their part in the World Wars. We may experience life at sea aboard Grand Banks fishing schooners, mackerel seiners, oyster boats and whalers. Cargo ships. Pilot boats. Merchant vessels. Immigrant ships. Those pressed into the slave trade. There is not a chapter of our history which does not have a waterborne link. The smell of pine tar and manila, the sounds of a working ship, the view of a whale-spotted horizon from the top of the rig, the motion of a rolling deck — history is a compelling study in this physical context.

Other North American ships sail ambassadorial missions for the public they serve, issuing invitations of hospitality and promoting opportunities for economic development. Other sail to save the environment. Or to promote international relations through citizen diplomacy, as did a Soviet-American crew sailing past the final sputters of the Cold War. These vessels draw our attention and focus us on their missions because sailing ships are powerful icons, symbolizing strength, beauty and harmony wherever they go. Those who sail know the ocean to be that which connects us to foreign lands — not a boundary which separates us.

Several American sail training ships serve as residential treatment centers for adjudicated youth while others provide exclusive corporate team building exercise or offshore adventure travel — from coastal cruising with gourmet cooking to blue water voyaging. While the clientele could not be more different, these ships are all in the business of enrichment.

As diverse an agenda as this may seem at first glance, these ships *all* provide sail training. The common denominator is that each uses wind and sea to teach us something else. Sail training, like reading, is not a subject in and of itself. It is a means to an end. A medium. An environment. We at ASTA often say that sail training is not learning *to* sail, it is learning *from* sailing. From the ship, from the sea and perhaps most importantly, from yourself.

A ship at sea has been described as a microcosm of the planet. Resources are finite, waste must be managed responsibly and success depends on one's ability to work as a team. One quickly learns that many hands lighten a load. In a similar way, so do good shipmates — those who are focused, considerate, and good humored. There is no place on earth which better illuminates leadership qualities, nor marks the path so clearly toward achieving them. The rewards of a smoothly run ship are immediate, obvious and sweetly satisfying. As sailors have said for centuries, take care of your ship and she'll take care of you.

There is no better feeling in the world than coming off an early morning watch having watched the sun rise and helped to scrub everything down for the start of a new day. As you leave the ship in the hands of the next watch you realize how happy you are to see them — and even happier to leave them to it – as you go below for the sort of breakfast you'd never eat ashore and a grateful climb into a narrow berth assuming any angle of heel. Adjusting to sleeping when you can is strangely easy, and you find yourself sleeping easily in your bunk no matter the time of day or the weather (well, with the occasional notable exception!). You find yourself frequently aware of living completely in the moment, and you take great pride in accomplishing tasks and seeking new challenges for yourself.

Aboard a sail training vessel, as in life, our small piece is a critical part of the whole. The quality of our work, and the spirit in which we do it, has a profound effect on the well-being of everyone else aboard. Leadership, paradoxically, is arrived at by learning to take direction. Becoming a team player. Pulling your share of the load. Being absolutely responsible. Dependable. And, learning to depend on the responsibility of others. For no matter what the particular mission of a ship might be, it is essential that she be safely navigated and handsomely attended.

This is true of the larger world, but in that larger world, the quality of our actions are not so immediately apparent. In our day to day lives, most of us do not have at hand accessible evidence of collisions we've safely avoided, environmental conditions we gained advantage from, or courses accurately steered no matter the conditions. Our actions seem at times to be in a vacuum and feedback is often clouded by other issues. It often takes years to measure the efficacy of our navigation and our ability to "hand, reef and steer" our lives. Nor do we often have the simple yet somehow completely thrilling affirmation of perfectly set sails in a stiff breeze and a ship "with a bone in her teeth". On a sail training vessel, it's right there. Right now.

For some, sail training offers first time successes. For others, it is a much needed refresher course in life when we find ourselves, for instance, knocking hats off passersbys or staring too long at funeral processions — which Herman Melville describes as "high time to get to sea" in *Moby Dick*. For all, sail training offers an absolutely unique learning experience.

So, no, we don't just teach sailing. The ships illustrated in this book foster opportunities for intensive personal development — intensive life experience in order to advance leadership development, an utter reverence for nature, a sense of time and place, an appreciation for history, and teamwork ability. Sail training really teaches the qualities of stewardship, resourcefulness, pride, humility, bravery, strength and grace. And we learn to sail, too.

Pamela C. Wuerth
Executive Director
September 1996

Baltimore

a world class harbor

Photo: Thad Koza

BALTIMORE'S OFFICIAL
COMMITTEE ON VISITING
SHIPS

SAIL BALTIMORE

1997-98
THE WHITBREAD

THE WHITBREAD
ROUND THE WORLD RACE
COMES TO BALTIMORE
APRIL 1998

Pride
OF BALTIMORE II

B·A·L·T·I·M·O·R·E
200
1797 · AMERICA'S CITY OF FIRSTS · 1997

Living Classrooms Foundation
LADY MARYLAND

For information, call 800·282·6632

A Brief History of the American Sail Training Association

The American Sail Training Association (ASTA) was founded in 1973 by the late Barclay Warburton, owner of the brigantine *Black Pearl*, as an affiliate of the Sail Training Association — now the International Sail Training Association (ISTA) — to coordinate and conduct sail training activities in American waters.

Initially ASTA worked to coordinate races and gatherings of sail training ships around the United States.

ASTA is just one of the many national sail training associations that developed in the wake of ISTA's success in gathering a small fleet, now grown dramatically, of traditional square-riggers for friendly exchange and competition. ISTA's international Tall Ships[®] races, with designated harbor festivals, bring together the ships and shores of most European countries, Russia and the former Soviet states, Canada, Mexico, and countries throughout South America and around the Pacific Ocean, including Australia, New Zealand, Indonesia and Japan.

ASTA's interest in helping to establish and codify standards for sail training ships and programs developed rapidly with the formation of the Council of Educational Ship Owners, which lobbied successfully for the passage of the Sailing School Vessels Act of 1982. The Sailing School Vessels Council, founded in the following year, worked with the US Coast Guard to develop regulations for sailing school vessels.

Tall Ships® Newport '92 Rally Awards Ceremony
ASTA file photo

In conjunction with the Australian Bicentenary Tall Ships[®] gathering in Sydney, ASTA also organized the first international discussion on safety standards and equipment for sail training programs. This was followed by the first safety at sea seminars in 1989. The seminars were modeled on the United States Sailing Association's seminars, but adapted for programs on particular aspects of sailing safety. As these sessions grew more specific to the sail training industry, the name was changed to Safety Under Sail Seminars.

As an alternative to racing, ASTA developed the concept of rallying sail training vessels where various aspects of seamanship can be demonstrated underway and ashore. Rallies frequently occur at various locations with a variety of ASTA vessels participating.

In addition, ASTA has worked with the ISTA and other national sail training associations in the organization of sail training races and cruises-in-company in connection with international events of major significance. Among those have been:

1976	The Tall Ships® Races from Bermuda to Newport prior to the celebration of the United States Bicentennial at Operation Sail 1976 in New York.
1978	The first sail training race in the Pacific Rim, held in honor of the voyages of Captain James Cook.
1979	The first National Maritime Heritage Week, held in Newport Rhode Island.
1980	Celebration of Boston's 350th Anniversary.
1984	ASTA/ISTA Tall Ships® Races held in honor of the 450th Anniversary of Jacques Cartier's first voyage to Canada, coordinated with the Canadian Sail Training Association (CSTA), founded the same year.
1986	Cruises-in-Company held in conjunction with transatlantic races to Operation Sail 1986/Salute to Liberty in honor of the Statue of Liberty's centennial.
1990	The first Tall Ships® Rally in Chesapeake Bay.
1992	Rallies in conjunction with the Christopher Columbus Quincentenary.
1994	Sail Toronto, Tall Ships® Erie, and ASTA's first Great Lakes Rally.
1995	Tall Ships® Race and Rally in cooperation with Mystic Seaport.
1996	ASTA and ISTA form Joint Venture to organize North American component of Tall Ships 2000®.

Over the years, ASTA has also undertaken many other projects to meet the needs of the rapidly growing sail training community. These include publications, conferences and seminars.

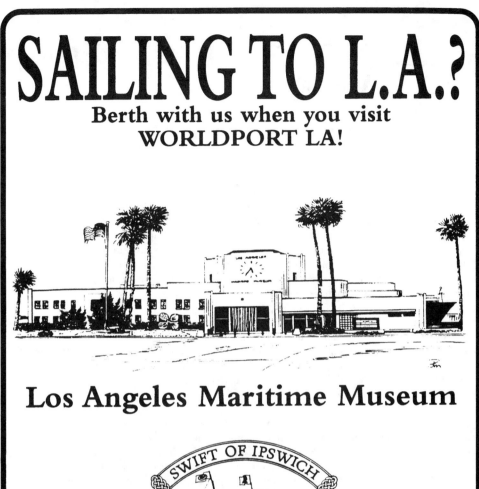

ASTA Programs
and Professional Services

From the first, **ASTA's Annual Conference** has gathered a broad spectrum of educators, ships' masters, port representatives, public officials, marine suppliers, naval architects, program administrators, festival managers, preservationists, environmentalists and crew. Conference sessions are developed in response to evaluations and input from ASTA members as well as outside trends. Sessions are structured to provide an open forum for information exchange, with a panel of experts to guide the discussion and to answer questions from the floor. In addition to such topics as vessel operations, regulatory issues, educational programming, and safety at sea, conference sessions have addressed media relations, marketing, funding and other non-profit management issues.

Through the **International Safety Forum**, initiated in 1992 in cooperation with the ISTA, ASTA works to expand the international dialogue among professional mariners by collecting and discussing case studies of actual incidents at sea and from these developing workable safety strategies. The Forum and its annually published proceedings are highly recommended for all professionals engaged in sail training, sea education, vessel operations, and tall ship events from throughout the world.

One of ASTA's chief concerns has always been to ensure that the highest safety standards are maintained by all those who participate in sail training programs, whether as officers, crew, instructors, or trainees. ASTA's **Safety Under Sail Seminars** focus on safety and survival issues for sail training programs. Through this innovative lecture and hands-on approach to safety issues, ASTA provides the opportunity for captains, crew, and program developers to improve their instructional and operational skills.

The **American Sail Training Association Marine Insurance Program** provides organizational and supporting members of ASTA the ability to secure comprehensive insurance at a very competitive price. The program is specifically designed to provide commercial insurance for all hull and liability risks of vessels, whether they are navigating, permanently berthed, or under construction. The program includes benefits such as personal effects coverage for crew and trainees, separate deductibles for theft of electronics, and extension of liability coverage for piers, docks, and ticket areas. The ASTA Marine Insurance Program is underwritten by Lloyds of London through the Crawley Warren Group, a Lloyds of London broker and Commercial Union Insurance Co., a US company.

For further information regarding the ASTA Insurance Program, contact David Markell at Hansen Marine Associates, Inc. (401) 848-9173.

As a service to professional members, ASTA maintains a **Billet Bank** through which experienced sailors (licensed or not) can be networked with ships in need of crew. ASTA members enrolled in the Billet Bank are required to complete a Billet Bank Registration which is kept on file at the ASTA office and highlights personal information, applicable licenses, edu-

ASTA provides sail training mariners with a variety of opportunities for professional development through Safety Under Sail Seminars, the International Safety Forum and the Annual Conference on Sail Training and Tall Ships.

ASTA file photo

cation, marine experience, seatime, and specific interests.

When a vessel identifies a crew requirement to the ASTA office, names and phone numbers of qualified Billet Bank members are provided to the ship and the opening is published in the next quarterly issue of *Running Free*. Any future contact between the vessels and applicants is handled between the parties themselves as ASTA does not endorse any specific program or individual, but simply shares information as it becomes available.

See page 202 for a Billet Bank Registration form. (You must be a member of ASTA to register. Join us today!)

No Additives.
No Preservatives.
Just Hood Quality.

The best sails begin with the best components. Hood's secret to producing great, long lasting cruising sails begins with the cloth. You see, at Hood we produce our own cloth, insuring that it's the best you can buy. Hood pioneered the use of Dacron and we are still the only sailmaker weaving our own cloth. And, we guarantee worldwide service on all Hood products.

Our Dacron cloth is woven tighter. It's not dependent on resins for shape retention. For its weight, Hood sailcloth is more pure yarn, so it's soft, manageable, and will withstand even the harshest elements. Hood now offers cruising sails made from Ultra Spectra - our Dacron reinforced with Spectra® - for added strength and longevity.

The pride we have in producing our cloth is carried into the design of your sail. Our HoodNet software links Hood cloth characteristics to sail design, laser cutting, and manufacturing. This advanced technology assists us in creating the correct shape for your cruising sails.

Quality is the backbone of our craftsmanship. Every seam is stitched with our trademark ultra violet resistant brown thread. Corners are reinforced with either Hood rings or hand-stitched leather clad patches. Each batten pocket is fortified from the inside out with extra layers of fabric.

Hood sails have cruised more miles around the world than any other brand of sails. Our commitment to quality service has been our trademark in sailmaking since our beginning. Hood lofts are located in every corner of the world, to service you and your sails, wherever you cruise.

Hood sails are controlled from the first fiber to the final hand-stitch. Pure quality. No additives. No preservatives. That's why Hood remains the most trusted name in sailmaking.

The Trusted Name in Sailmaking.

HOOD
SAILMAKERS

Hood Corporate
200 High Point Avenue
Portsmouth, RI 02871
800-688-4660

HOOD EUROPE
Bath Road
Lymington, Hants SO41 3RW
England 44-1-590-675-011

HOOD TEXTILES
McCurtain Hill
Clonakilty, County Cork
Ireland 353-23-33406

HOOD SAILMAKERS WORLDWIDE

COSTA MESA, CALIFORNIA 714-548-3464, SAN FRANCISCO, CALIFORNIA 415-332-4104
NONAK, CONNECTICUT 203-572-9547, CLEARWATER, FLORIDA 813-461-1926
FT. LAUDERDALE, FLORIDA 305-522-4663, PORTLAND, MAINE 207-828-0003
ANNAPOLIS, MARYLAND 410-268-4663, ORIENTAL, NORTH CAROLINA 919-249-2093
TORONTO, ONTARIO 905-625-1789, ST. THOMAS, VIRGIN ISLANDS 809-775-6060

ARGENTINA AUSTRALIA GERMANY ITALY JAPAN MALLORCA
MALTA NETHERLANDS PERU SPAIN SWEDEN

ASTA Publications

Running Free is ASTA's newsletter which all members receive on a quarterly basis. Among the standard features appearing in *Running Free* are articles on conferences, rallies, legislation and regulations affecting sail training, as well as news about ships and ports, and announcements of employment opportunities.

The ASTA directory, now entitled *Sail Tall Ships! A Directory of Sail Training and Adventure at Sea,* first appeared in 1980, and is now in its ninth edition. The directory provides information about ASTA and its goals, and details on scores of sail training ships and programs in the United States and Canada, as well as affiliated sail training associations throughout the world. The directory is provided to all current ASTA members and additional copies of the directory are available through the ASTA office. To help fulfill ASTA's mission, the directory is also distributed through maritime museums and their affiliated shops, marinas, Tall Ships events, and sail training programs, as well as bookstores, libraries, high school guidance counselors, university career resource centers, and education conferences throughout the United States and Canada.

Shenandoah from aloft.
George Ancona photo

ASTA *Guidelines for Educational Programs Under Sail* defines ASTA standards for sail training education within the framework of the Sailing School Vessels Act. This manual defines criteria and indicators of effectiveness for the design, delivery, and evaluation of curricula, instruction, and program administration. In addition to the core of safe seamanship education, the guidelines apply to all aspects of sail training: adventure, education, environmental science, maritime heritage, and leadership development.

The ASTA *Syllabus and Logbook* provides a progression of skill-building activities in nautical and marine science: safety; seamanship; navigation; and oceanography. This pocket-size outline enables trainees to keep a personal log of their sea time and to document their progress in sail training. Requirements for the syllabus are carefully spelled out, and completion of course work and sea time must be certified by either the instructor or the ship's master.

The *International Safety Forum Proceedings*, the annual publication of the International Safety Forum, is provided to all participants and attendees. It has become highly recommended reading for all professionals engaged in sail training, sea education, and vessel operation and is available through the ASTA office. The Forum addresses topics ranging from the theoretical to the practical: the need to balance safety and challenge in sail training operations, underway mishaps and lessons learned, hypothermia, crew training, safety drills, and designing sail training vessels and programs with safety in mind.

Tall Ships 2000® Official Schedule

Europe –

> Southampton, England, Wednesday 29 March - Saturday 1 April
>
> Genoa, Italy Wednesday 29 March - Saturday 1 April

Race 1 **Start – Southampton** *and* **Genoa, Finish – Agadir**

> **Africa –**
>
> Agadir, Morocco, Tuesday 18 April - Friday 21 April

Race 2 **Start – Africa, Finish – North America**

> **North America –**
>
> First Trans-Atlantic Race Finish Port, Friday 26 May - Monday 29 May*
>
> Rally Port 1, Friday 9 June - Monday 12 June*
>
> Rally Port 2, Friday 23 June - Monday 26 June*
>
> Boston, Wednesday 12 July - Sunday 16 July

Race 3 **Start – Boston, Finish – Canada**

> Second Trans-Atlantic Race Start Port, Friday 21 July - Sunday 24 July*

Race 4 **Start – US or Canada, Finish – Amsterdam, Holland**

> **Europe –**
>
> Amsterdam, Holland, Saturday 19 August - Tuesday 22 August*

* Dates are proposed and subject to selection of additional North American Ports.

Tall Ships 2000®

Tall Ships 2000® will be the largest gathering of Tall Ships in history. Hundreds of vessels from throughout the world will participate in off-shore sail training events linking the continents of Europe, Africa and North America. Ships and crews will gather in officially designated host ports between races for safety briefings and crew exchanges as well as celebration and ceremony. ASTA has joined the International Sail Training Association in organizing the North American part of the series of trans-oceanic and coastal races and cruises in company planned to celebrate the new millennium and to draw attention to sail training. ASTA and ISTA share a common objective for Tall Ships 2000®: to make the character-building values of sail training the foundation for world-class interest, enthusiasm and participation.

The official start of Tall Ships 2000® begins in early March of the year 2000 with simultaneous festivities in Southampton, England and Genoa, Italy. Parallel races from those ports finish in Agadir, Morocco where ships will provision and prepare for the first of two trans-Atlantic legs. From Africa, the ships will race to a Caribbean port and then begin a

The aim of the International Sail Training Association is "To enable young people of all nations to race together at sea." Because of the very wide range of sailing vessels which take part in the races they organize, the ISTA has developed a rating system which allows single-masted sloops to compete against four-masted barks. Parade of Sail La Caruna. Sedov *leading.*

Janka Bielak photo

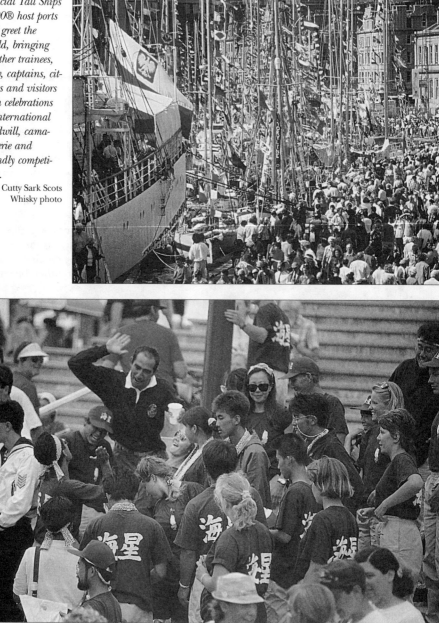

Official Tall Ships 2000® host ports will greet the world, bringing together trainees, crew, captains, citizens and visitors with celebrations of international goodwill, camaraderie and friendly competition.
Cutty Sark Scots Whisky photo

In addition to meeting the challenge of racing together at sea, trainees will have opportunities to participate in crew exchanges, gaining further experience of ships as well as contemporaries of other nationalities.
ASTA file photo

Ships from throughout the world will participate in a series of trans-Atlantic and coastal races, linking ports on the continents of Europe, Africa and North America. Parades of Sail and other special shore-side events are planned to capture the attention and excitement of the media and ultimately the public — future sailors and supporters of sail training!
ASTA file photo

cruise in company north, stopping in various US ports along the way, to two Rally Ports (undetermined as this *Directory* goes to press) , where they will gather for official reception and ASTA/ISTA -sanctioned events. Boston is the first North American port to be designated an official host of Tall Ships 2000®, and we look forward to a repeat of the successful event enjoyed there in 1992.

From Boston, the vessels will join in a Race to the Canadian Maritimes, with an expectation of the largest number of Race entries in the series, as the European fleet is joined by those of South America, the Pacific and North America. It is expected that a Canadian port will host the last official North American event of Tall Ships 2000®, where the ships will prepare for the final leg of the event: a trans-Atlantic Race to finish in Amsterdam, Holland.

Thousands of participants and millions of visitors can be expected to visit the fleet during officially-scheduled port visits. The appeal of Class-A Tall Ships, such as the US Coast Guard's barque *Eagle,* and hundreds of other ships sailing from around the world, will provide host ports a unique opportunity for celebration against the backdrop of the majestic spectacle of the ships.

Even more important, although perhaps less visible, will be the gathering of trainees from throughout the world as they meet their peers in the spirit of friendly competition and international camaraderie. The Tall Ships' dual mission of diplomatic service and the development of leadership qualities in those who train aboard offers the ideal atmosphere for exchange and cooperation and the opportunity to foster international friendship and understanding.

Tall Ships 2000® is first and foremost a sail training event. It is a combination of off-shore events organized for the benefit of sail training vessels and crews. ASTA and the International Sail Training Association are both equally dedicated to supporting opportunities for the development of leadership skills, personal growth, hands-on education, positive international interaction, friendly competition and camaraderie through the challenge of the sea.

Choosing a Sail Training Program

The four essential components of any sail training program are a seaworthy vessel, a competent captain and crew, qualified instructors, and a sound educational program appropriate and suited for the trainee's needs.

There are as many sail training programs as there are ships, and choosing the right one depends a great deal on your personal needs and desires. Sail training differs from going on a cruise ship, in that you are *expected* to take part in the running of the ship by handling sail and line, standing watch, and working in the galley (the ship's kitchen). Whether you want a program that specializes in oceanography or adventure travel, one that lasts a day, a week, or an entire semester, whether you want to ship out in a schooner, or whether you want the added challenge and thrill of climbing aloft in a square rigger; these options will ultimately dictate the type of program a prospective trainee may choose. As to what sail training programs require of the trainee, beyond an eager willingness to get the most out of their time on the water, the requirements are few.

Many ASTA *member vessels work with schools in order to offer academic credit for time spent at sea.*

Roger Archibald photo

Safety Trainees should look for vessels that operate under US Coast Guard regulations. Many ships venture no more than 20 miles from a harbor and are rarely underway overnight. Offshore voyaging offers the challenge of distant passages where severe weather and water conditions may be unavoidable. Being underway round the clock requires watch duties night and day, demanding both physical and mental stamina and perseverance. If applying to a foreign flag vessel, look into the international regulations that apply.

Sailing Experience With few exceptions, no prior experience is required of trainees, although a high degree of competency must be demonstrated for anyone seeking volunteer or paid crew positions.

Swimming ability Trainees are encouraged to be able to stay afloat for at least five minutes while fully dressed, however most programs have no formal swimming requirements.

Age limits These vary from program to program, but most sail training programs start accepting unaccompanied trainees from the age of 14 (ninth grade).

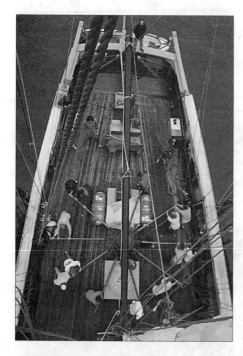

Left: Crew aboard the Niagara *perform many of the same duties as those who sailed the original brig in the War of 1812.*

ASTA file photo

Lower Left: Furling square sails aboard the "HMS" Rose. Going aloft is not for everyone! Most vessels do not require you do so, but many trainees find it to be an exciting part of life under-way.

Starke Jett photo

Below: Celestial navigation is taught aboard many ASTA member vessels. Although many ships are traditionally rigged and crewed, many have state of the art electronic navigational aids as well as compass and sextant.

George Ancona photo

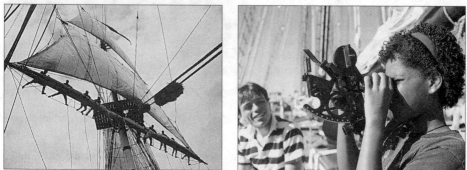

Academic credit Some vessels are tied directly to academic institutions that grant academic credit to trainees who successfully complete sail training programs as part of a course of study or project in a wide range of subjects. Some educational institutions will also grant credit for on-board independent study.

Co-education Some vessels sail with single gender crews; others are co-educational.

Cost Prices vary considerably, with the range being about $25 to $150 per person per day, depending on the nature and the duration of the program and the type of vessel.

Financial aid While a few vessels have limited financial assistance available, most trainees find it necessary to seek private, business, and/or community support to help defray the cost of sail training. In addition, there are a small number of independent organizations that provide financial aid to trainees, usually through matching grants.

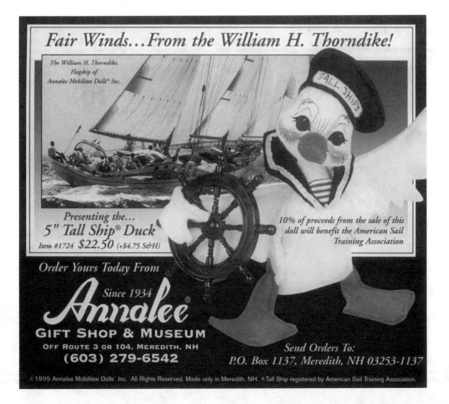

Sail Training Vessels

The sail training mission differs from vessel to vessel according to the type of program offered and the type of lessons to be learned. While the curriculum taught aboard any given vessel can vary from year to year, or from voyage to voyage, the scope of a ship's mission is determined in part by the type of vessel it is, as defined by government regulations written and enforced by the US Coast Guard (USCG). Some vessels carry dual certification. What follows is a brief description of the various types of program-related regulations.

Sail training is adventure travel under sail! Pictured is the schooner Bowdoin, Inukayaisat Passage, West Greenland (Lat. 71° N), *August 1994.*

Tom Stewart photo

Sailing School Vessels (SSV) are certified as Subchapter R — Nautical Schools — under Title 46 of the Code of Federal Regulations (CFR). A SSV is a vessel of less than 500 gross tons carrying six or more sailing school students or instructors, principally propelled by sail, and operated by a non-profit educational organization exclusively for the purpose of sailing education. Sailing School Vessels are required to pass regular inspection by the USCG in order to maintain their certification.

Passenger Vessels are certified according to size and number of passengers carried under Title 46 of the CFR:

Subchapter C— Uninspected (by the USCG) vessels which operate with no more than six passengers for hire.

Subchapter T— Small passenger vessels of under 100 gross tons that carry passengers for hire and are required to pass regular USCG inspection of the ship and all onboard equipment.

Subchapter K— Small passenger vessels of under 100 gross tons that carry more than 150 passengers for hire and are required to pass regular USCG inspection of the ship and all onboard equipment.

Subchapter H— Passenger vessels more than 100 gross tons that carry passengers for hire and are required to pass regular USCG inspection of the ship and all onboard equipment.

Because passenger vessels are technically engaged in trade or commerce, they   cannot operate under a certificate of inspection as SSVs. However, they are required to meet the highest USCG rules and regulations for the service in which they are engaged. Many offer educational programs and work closely with local community and education groups. They also provide excellent opportunities for sea experience, especially for those experienced trainees qualified to sign-on as volunteers or paid crew, as many do.

Attraction Vessels generally are museum ships tied up to a dock, usually, but not always, on a permanent basis. Although an attraction vessel's operators are entitled to charge admission to visitors or fees for programs conducted while the ship is at dock, attraction vessels may not charge trainees, passengers, or guests for any use of the vessel underway. The USCG inspection certifies their safety for dockside programs only.

Oceanographic Research Vessel (ORV) are certified as Subchapter U under Title 46 of the CFR. An ORV is a vessel employed exclusively in either oceanographic (saltwater) or limnologic (freshwater) instruction and/or research. ORVs generally will not hire any instructors without proper credentials. ORVs are inspected and certified by the USCG for ORV service.

Take Charge
of Your Sail Training Experience
Michael J. Rauworth

Take Charge of Your Sail Training Experience! As you think about a sail training experience, it is important to recognize who has responsibility for what, and especially what is your responsibility. One of the most important products of sail training is the development of a sense of judgment about what and whom you can rely on, and to what degree. This applies to: the compass, the weather forecast, your shipmates, the depths on the chart, the strength of the anchor cable, the vigilance of the lookout on the other ship, and many other things. Sail training also builds a reasoned sense of self-reliance. All of this starts from the moment you begin to think about a voyage.

At the helm of Tabor Boy, *owned and operated by Tabor Academy.*
Roger Archibald photo

Recognize who you are dealing with and what is included. When you book a sail training trip, you are dealing with the vessel owner, or its representatives — ASTA is not involved. You must evaluate whether the financial and business arrangements make sense for you. If there is connecting travel involved, for example, find out if you must make the arrangements, or if they are somehow tied into those you make with the vessel. What happens if you miss your ship because your plane is delayed, or vice versa? Do you need trip insurance? Have you confirmed with the vessel owner any possible customs or immigration issues? Will you need a passport or a pre-purchased air ticket? You must seek out the answers to these questions.

Make informed, responsible decisions about risk and safety, level of challenge, physical suitability and other important issues. One of the important reasons to embark on a sail training trip is to engage the world in a different, stimulating, and challenging way — if you want to stay warm and dry, you should stay at home by the fireplace. Much of the point is to come face-to-face with the elements. At the very least, this probably means that you will find yourself wet, chilled, or tired at some point in a challenging voyage. But everyone's threshold for this is different, and you need to find out what you are likely to be experiencing in order to find out if it is well matched for you.

Since the beginning of time, going to sea has been recognized as carrying an element of risk. These days, we more commonly think about risk in connection with highway travel or aviation, but the idea is the same: you get a pre-flight safety brief on an airliner, you get a lifeboat drill on a cruise ship. Part of the value of sail training is addressing these issues head on. You need to decide whether you are comfortable with the combination of risks and safety measures connected with your proposed sail training trip.

For example, will you be able to go aloft? Will trips in smaller craft be involved? Will you be expected to stand watch at night? Do the demands of the ship match your physical and health capabilities? Are you on medication that will (or may) become necessary during the voyage, or do you have a condition (for example, hemophilia or epilepsy) that may require special access to medical attention; if so, is the vessel operator aware of this? Will you be able to get up and down the ladders, in and out of your berth, and along a heeled-over deck? If there is an emergency, will you be needed to handle safety equipment or to help operate the vessel?

Remember that sail training is often not intended to be like a vacation. Some vessels, on the other hand, may offer leisurely voyages, where very little will be asked of you. You should

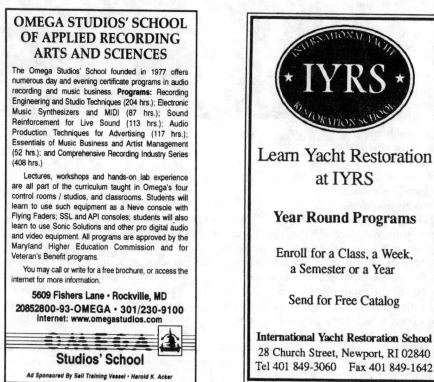

arrive at a clear understanding of these issues prior to setting sail.

In short, you must satisfy yourself that the trip you are looking into is the right thing for you to do, considering safety, risk, suitability, challenge, comfort, convenience, educational value, cost, and any other factors you consider important.

Does ASTA have a hand in any of this? In a word — no! ASTA is your "bulletin board" to introduce you to opportunities. However, ASTA does not operate any vessels, and has no ability or authority to inspect, approve, or even recommend vessels or programs because programs are constantly evolving and changing.

ASTA is a non-profit group with a limited staff. It serves as a forum for the sail training community, but it has no authority over what programs are offered, nor how vessels are operated. The information in this directory is supplied by the vessel operators, and ASTA can not possibly verify all the information, nor visit all the ships in order to evaluate programs. For these reasons, you must take the information in this directory as a starting point only, subject to change and correction, and proceed directly with the vessel operator. ASTA is not an agent or business partner for the vessel operators, and is not a travel agent.

ASTA believes in the value of sail training as a concept, but remember, from the moment you step beyond looking at this book, the decision and the resulting experiences rest with you.

Michael J. Rauworth is a current member of the ASTA Board of Directors, an attorney, and a life-long sailor.

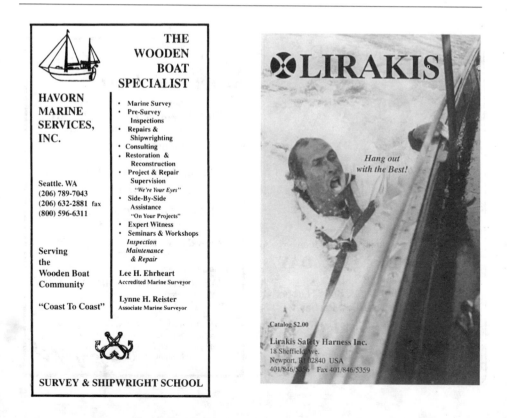

Shipping Out

What follows is an abbreviated version of a memorandum sent to all volunteers who ship out aboard the U. S. Brig *Niagara*. The brig *Niagara* is a museum ship – her below decks living area is authentic to a ship of the early 19th century. Each ship has its own living arrangements, rules and requirements, and trainees should inquire about specific gear before signing on, as well as the type of USCG certification and route the ship has been inspected for.

Suggestions for packing before you ship out...
Please remember that your personal space on board is very limited. Be conservative in the amount of gear you pack! All your gear must be stowed in your seabag. Excessive gear will only mean discomfort for you. No suitcases or bulky backpacks; put all gear in a canvas, sea, or duffel bag.

Bedding
The *Niagara* supplies a hammock and a place to hang it. You should bring sheets, blankets, a pillow, or a sleeping bag.

Life at sea presents new and different challenges. ASTA member vessels offer a variety of programs to get underway — for a day, a week or more.

Sail, Inc. photo

Gear
Dress for the program is informal. Follow the **Gear List** when you are packing for the voyage. Bring old clothes as some of your belongings may well get permanently stained.

Foul Weather Gear
Good quality yellow or orange gear and rubber knee-high seaboots with heels are highly recommended. Ponchos, poplin raincoats, flat-soled shoes, and cheap plastic gear are pretty useless onboard a vessel.

Clothes
Rugged work clothes are best. No special shoes required. Sneakers are fine. We suggest long polypropylene underwear for warmth.

Money
You will not be able to cash personal checks. We recommend you bring sufficient but appropriate money in the form of travelers checks. It is very difficult to secure funds after the ship leaves port.

Climate
Be prepared for rain, warm, and cool temperatures. Bring some warm clothes for the ship as offshore temperatures can be quite cool. Be prepared for exposure to the sun.

Meals at sea are hearty! Pictured is the gracious salon aboard the topsail schooner Shenandoah, *which sails from Martha's Vineyard.*

George Ancona photo

Equipment
Feel free to bring a musical instrument, camera, and other or sound recording equipment. NO portable radios, boom boxes, walkmans, cell phones, tape players, or pre-recorded tapes are allowed on board.

Laundry
On short voyages, save it for the end of the trip. On longer trips, either do it ashore or with a scrub brush, buckets of water, and biodegradable detergent on deck at approved times.

Suggested Gear List

· Sunglasses
· Sunscreen lotion
· Sun hat
· 2 pair of dungarees or work-type pants
· 3 or 4 T-shirts
· Cool weather clothes (jackets, gloves, or watch caps)
· Foul weather gear (jacket, pants, and overalls)
· Rigging knife
· Sneakers
· Light sweater
· Long underwear (2 to 3 changes)
· Insect repellent
· Small waterproof flashlight and batteries
· Saltwater soap and shampoo (Prell and/or Lemon Fresh Joy)
· Bathing suit
· Toilet articles
· Bath towel, hand towel, wash cloth
· Warm socks, (2 pair - light and heavy)
· Rubber boots (knee-high) heeled
· Canvas, sea, or duffel bag
· Shore-going clothes and footwear, a small daypack
· Camera with protective covering, film (optional)
· Writing materials (1 exercise book, 2 pencils)

You may sail to discover the waterfront in your own community or on a bluewater adventure of a lifetime...
Bill Grant for
"HMS" Rose Foundation photo

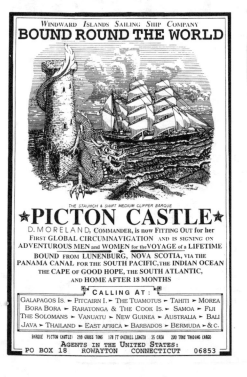

High school and college students may find accredited programs aboard ships like the Westward, *operated by Sea Education Association of Woods Hole, Massachusetts.*

Halden Jensen photo

SEA SSV Westward

Halden Jensen

From the moment we started hoisting our sails, I knew my week on the *Westward* would be unlike anything I'd experienced before. As I climbed out on the bowsprit to undo the stops on the jib and topsail, I felt the unfamiliar thrill of trying to balance while rising and plunging through the air. As I shouted with my friends and fellow students, I felt the struggle of teamwork. And when the sails were set and we were pushing smoothly along by the stiff breeze, I could marvel at the intense pleasure I derived from work, cooperation, beauty, and learning.

I learned every day (and every night, for the boat never sleeps) I spent on the *Westward*. I learned the difference between standing and running rigging, how to tie a bowline, and what it means to "heave to". I learned the principles of navigation, and will never forget the time the watch officer asked me to figure out what course to steer for the night. I operated a hydrowinch to take a water sample and probe the ocean. Through oxygen, temperature, salinity, phosphate, and a myriad of other tests, I measured and analyzed the unending blue around me. I also learned to scrub soles and cook in a cramped galley on a pitching ship. These practical aspects of life at sea were often the most difficult to learn.

It was the practical part of daily living that made the experience such a challenging, and in the end, a rewarding one. While food was plentiful, sleep was not. In one 24-hour period, I saw the sunrise, sunset, and moonset. A freshwater rinse was a luxury, and my personal space was a six by three by four foot bunk. Yet, it was easy to forget the discomforts and become totally absorbed in the ship and the sea. I felt stronger in the knowledge that I wasn't dependent upon the niceties of my "normal" life.

I was, however, very dependent upon everyone else aboard the ship, as they were upon me. No one person, no mater how competent, could set and strike sail, steer and navigate a 125-foot staysail schooner, let alone collect scientific data, cook, clean, and monitor the engine room. There were certainly quarrels and complaints among the students, but we were forced to work through them. I had to place my trust in every person to do what was necessary to insure a safe and productive voyage. And by virtue of their trust in me, I worked hard to complete my small tasks in order for the whole to function. On all of my sports teams or in all of my clubs, I have never been such an integral part, and have never felt such an atmosphere of teamwork as aboard the *Westward*.

On the evening before we returned to port, we anchored for the night. As we sailed into the bay, the crew stepped back and told the students to drop sail. Comfortable with what had been alien objects days ago, I furled the jib. I was yelling and being yelled at simultaneously and chaos seemed to reign supreme. Then the confusion passed and the sails were down. The captain was congratulating us on a job well-done. Smiling at my friends, I relaxed to watch the sun spread its light across the water before sinking below the waves.

Halden Jensen is from McLean, Virginia. As a high school student, Halden spent three weeks aboard the Westward *studying oceanography in the Gulf of Maine during the summer of 1993.*

Reflections
on the Film *White Squall*

Nancy Richardson

Few people know of the Girl Scout legacy in the true story behind the movie *White Squall*. It really struck me when I realized that there were five generations of Mariner Girl Scouts drawn to the theater the afternoon I first saw the film!

Why were we all there? Because it is the story of another Mariner Girl Scout, Dr. Alice Strahan Sheldon, who was a member of the Maplewood, New Jersey, Mariner Girl Scout "ship" (as Mariner troops are known) in the late 1940s. Some of us knew Alice only through her letters and pictures in the troop scrapbooks. Like Alice, all of us had our lives touched by being connected with that special Girl Scout troop. Like millions of other Girl Scouts, we developed self-potential and values, related to others, and did community service. But, unlike most Girl Scouts, we had the extraordinary advantage of learning in the very special environment of a sailing ship, as did the boys aboard the Sheldons' schooner *Albatross*.

After Girl Scout community service as a teen volunteer at Orange Orthopedic Hospital, Alice became a physician and went on to sail as ship's doctor on the seventh world voyage with Irving and Exy Johnson aboard their brigantine *Yankee*. Alice and Chris Sheldon, *Yankee*'s first mate, were married soon after their return in 1959. Soon thereafter, they launched their own school ship program aboard the steel-hulled schooner, *Albatross*. Their dream came to a tragic end in the white squall that took Alice and five others down with the ship two years later.

Most people see sailing as a romantic escape into the sunset. Instead, the movie shows how on a ship, "beyond the blue horizon" we really come face-to-face with our selves. "Knowing the ropes" means being able pull together with our shipmates physically, mentally, and emotionally. Although the spirit of Girl Scouting comes alive in many different ways, as Mariners we learned a deep sense of respect, responsibility and resourcefulness from sailing. We learned to "lean forward into the winds of life" from wonderful people like Skipper and Exy Johnson, aboard beautiful ships like *Yankee*. We learned that life is rarely more concentrated and authentic than on a ship under sail. I smile at the latest "ropes course" challenges set up in camps, for the original, uncontrived version is, indeed, a ship's rigging, where every line has a place and a purpose. So, too, the people.

Celebrating our 60th anniversary last year, the Maplewood ship is the oldest continuously active Mariner Girl Scout troop in the United States. We've been meeting since 1935, and we're still sailing! Last summer we were in the Tall Ships Parade for the Special Olympics and this year we'll get underway in June aboard the *Lettie G. Howard* out of South Street Seaport Museum, through the Girl Scout Council of Greater Essex County.

Critics called *White Squall* a boring "boys-to-men" adventure, exclusive, elitist and out of touch with contemporary issues. Yet this true story, taken from one boy's logbook, still resonates today. Log entries from my Girl Scout shipmates show that their sail training experiences taught them how to climb higher, pull harder and see further – beyond limited horizons into new worlds.

There are literally hundreds of Girl Scout sailing stories... and not just from the Maplewood Mariners. *White Squall* is both a memorial and a reminder of a tragic accident.

But we must never lose sight of the fact that sail training and Girl Scouting are rich and rewarding experiences that deeply touch many lives.

A long-time member and director of the American Sail Training Association, Nancy Richardson served as Co-Chairman of ASTA from 1987 to 1992. She is currently the Pluralism and Adult Development Counselor for the Girl Scouts of the USA in New York City.

The *Albatross*

Built in 1920 and originally named *Alk*, the *Albatross* began life as a North Sea pilot schooner. From 1949 to 1956 Royal Rotterdam Lloyd employed her as a training ship for future merchant ship officers. The Sheldons acquired the ship in 1959 and formed Ocean Academy, Inc., carrying up to fourteen students at a time. On May 3, 1961, while en route from Progreso, Mexico, to Nassau, the Bahamas, *Albatross* was hit by a white squall about 125 miles west of the Dry Tortugas. She sank almost instantly, taking with her Alice Sheldon, four students and the ship's cook. The tragic voyage was the subject of the feature film *White Squall*, released in 1996.

After the loss of *Albatross* the United States Coast Guard undertook a thorough review of the stability and design requirements for sailing school ships. ASTA contributed significantly to this effort, which resulted in passage of the Sailing School Vessels Act of 1982.

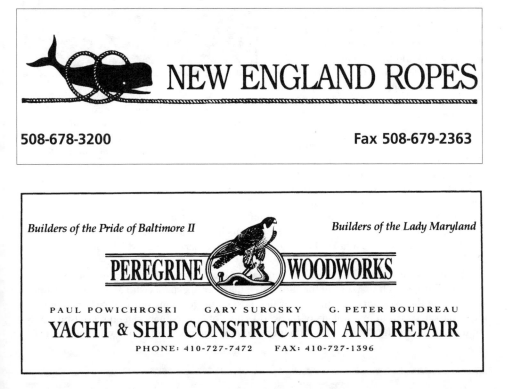

Sail Training: The Next Century

Captain David V. V. Wood

This article has previously appeared in *Sea History, Tall Ships News* and ASTA's 1995 *Directory of Sail Training Programs and Tall Ships*

In late July of 1972, the U.S. Coast Guard's training barque *Eagle* set sail from her home port of New London, Connecticut on an extraordinary voyage. In what amounted to a Presidential command performance, she was to participate in a Tall Ships Race from the Solent, on England's south coast, to the Skaw between Denmark and Sweden, and then visit Kiel, Germany for the sailing events of the 1972 Olympic Games–the first time she had returned to Germany since being taken over by the Coast Guard at Bremerhaven in 1946, in the aftermath of World War II. There were a number of other "firsts" for *Eagle* in this voyage, but they belong to another story. What stood out for me–and, I believe, for *Eagle's* entire complement of officers, crew, and cadets–were the excitement and adventure of participating in a historic international event, the thrill of pitting our developing skills as square-rigger sailors against those of the other magnificent, cadet-crewed vessels in the race (Germany's *Gorch Fock II* and Poland's *Dar Pomorza*), and the opportunity to mingle ashore with fellow seamen from the 15 nations and more than 60 sail training vessels participating in the event. None of us had ever experienced anything so exhilarating; we had known some great sailing in *Eagle*, of course, but in isolation. The international *camaraderie* of seafarers, the challenge and satisfaction of competition, the drama and pageantry of a major international gathering–these were new, and they were wonderfully exciting. It would not be an understatement to say that the

"...Such experiences of the thousands of people who go to see the ships and share in the excitement of the ports who host them, go a long way toward explaining the remarkable growth in numbers of the world's fleet of large, square-rigged schoolships during the late twentieth century."

ASTA file photo

experience set my own course for the remainder of my Coast Guard career, and while there were many glorious days during my subsequent tours in *Eagle* and other ships, I would frequently look back to 1972 as a kind of watershed, a benchmark against which such days were to be measured.

Such experiences on the part of the thousands of young people who participate in such events in Europe each year, not to mention the millions of spectators who go to see the ships and share in the excitement in the ports which host them, go a long way toward explaining the remarkable growth in numbers of the world's fleet of large, square-rigged schoolships during the late twentieth century. Given the trend in modern merchant and naval fleets toward

ever larger and more complex ships with ever
smaller and more technologically sophisticated
crews, this development could hardly have been
anticipated when the organizers of the first
International Tall Ships Race set out in 1956 to
bring together what they believed were the *last*
of the great square riggers still training young
men for careers at sea for a race across the Bay
of Biscay from Torbay to Lisbon. Five ships
entered that race, three of them Scandinavian
(*Danmark*, *Christian Radich*, and *Sørlandet*), one
Belgian (*Mercator*), and one Portuguese (*Sagres
I*). Eight years later, when the organizers of the
first "Operation Sail" in New York Harbor had a
similar idea (the race was separately organized), more than twice as many large ships
showed up–three of them (Germany's *Gorch
Fock II*, Argentina's *Libertad*, and Chile's

*ASTA races and rallies involve crews in various
forms of competition, both at sea and ashore,
emphasizing seamanship, safety and teamwork.
Pictured is the crew of Bill of Rights, First
Place, Sail Training Class, 1995 ASTA Tall
Ships Race.*

ASTA file photo

Esmeralda) of post-World War II build.[1] And by
1992, when the "Grand Regatta Columbus Quincentenary" visited various U.S. ports in commemoration of Columbus' voyage to the New World, fully 10 of the 24 naval and merchant
schoolships present had been built since 1964.

To those (and I am one) who believe that the modern square-rigged ship represents a
pinnacle of human achievement in appropriate technology, and that–notwithstanding the size
and complexity of modern oceangoing vessels–training at sea under sail remains the best possible sort of apprenticeship for those aspiring to a seagoing career, this growth in the number
of schoolships is indeed gratifying. But it must be acknowledged that the equally remarkable
growth in popularity of tall ships *events* has played a significant part in encouraging the
increase in large, traditionally-rigged schoolships. Tall ship gatherings on a grand scale, such
as 1992's Operation Sail and Sail Boston, are relatively infrequent in North America, for the
simple reason that only one large schoolship (the Coast Guard's *Eagle*) is based here, and
such ships tend to be tied fairly closely to an academic program that makes the scheduling of
transoceanic voyages difficult to coordinate with such events; but more modest gatherings of
traditionally rigged vessels, with an occasional large schoolship, have become a regular feature
of such annual festivals as Norfolk's "Harborfest" and similar harbor and waterfront celebrations around the country. And in Europe, the annual schedule of such events is almost bewildering, with port cities from Scandinavia to Iberia vying fiercely to host the scores of sailing
vessels competing each year in the "Cutty Sark Tall Ships Races"–direct descendants of that
first race in 1956.

The popularity of such events is not surprising. For all the obvious reasons–the desire to
celebrate a glorious maritime past, nostalgia for an age when human affairs moved at a slower
and less bewildering tempo, the romance of the sea and far-off, exotic places, admiration for
the craftsmanship and beauty of the ships themselves–people by the thousands and even millions are drawn to the waterfront whenever sailing ships are in harbor. In his foreword to
Operation Sail's official program for the 1992 event, OpSail's Honorary Chairman Walter
Cronkite suggests that we celebrate ships because they brought our world "to the critical pitch
of communication and commerce that has made today's global awareness possible." What-
ever the attraction, by bringing visitors to town, tall ships events inevitably provide an econom-

ic boost to the cities hosting them, and can even be a catalyst for waterfront redevelopment, improved facilities for tourism, and so forth. The Commonwealth of Massachusetts, for example estimated the overall economic impact of Sail Boston 1992 at something on the order of $500 million, and a study commissioned by the Merseyside Development Corporation, which organized events in the port of Liverpool for the final port call of the Grand Regatta Columbus, found benefits on a comparable scale. For the owners (usually governments) of large schoolships, such events are a marvelous opportunity for showing the flag and generating international goodwill, or even for subtly promoting economic investment in their countries– a fact which may help to explain why much of the recent growth in the number of large schoolships has been in such places as Latin America and Eastern Europe (including Russia). For the crews and trainees, of course, such events are a wonderful opportunity to meet, compete, and party with people of similar age and interests, and to learn more about other cultures.

The Sail Training Association (STA), established in the United Kingdom in 1956 to carry on the idea embodied in the International Tall Ships Race of that year, deserves much of the credit for these developments. As the races (and the in-port events that attended them) grew steadily in popularity, they provided a stimulus to the growth of numerous sail training projects within the UK, most of which–unlike the big schoolships–had little or nothing to do with training professional seafarers. Rather, they grew more or less directly out of the idea embodied in the first Outward Bound school established at Aberdovey, Wales in 1941, that an experience of seafaring under sail is ideally suited to develop qualities of courage, endurance, discipline, self-reliance, resourcefulness, teamwork, tolerance, and humility (to name only a few) in young people. In short, it is a nearly-ideal character molding experience. In the words of Lawrence Holt, the British shipping magnate who funded the Aberdovey project in collaboration with the legendary Kurt Hahn, father of the Outward Bound movement, it was to be "less a training *for* the sea than *through* the sea, and so benefit all walks of life."[2] This has continued to be the prevalent model for sail training programs in England, most of which stress the aims of character development and adventure rather than seamanship, and most of which, incidentally, operate much smaller vessels than the big schoolships. The Ocean Youth Club, for example, sails a fleet of 12 ketches up to 72' in length, with berths for a dozen trainees each on week-long cruises; the largest vessels in the UK are the STA's own schooners, *Malcolm Miller* and *Sir Winston Churchill,* 150' in length with berths for 39 trainees each on cruises of two to three weeks.[3]

Originally biennial events, the STA races are now held annually, and regularly rotate between the Baltic, North Sea, the Bay of Biscay, and occasionally the Mediterranean. The stated aim of the Races–called the "Cutty Sark Tall Ships Races" since 1972, in recognition of the STA's long and happy relationship with its corporate sponsor, Berry Bros. and Rudd– is "to enable young people of all nations to race together at sea under sail," and the genius of the STA has been to consistently keep the focus on the young people on board the ships. Using its proven ability to bring large numbers of ships–most of them small-to-medium in size, but generally with a liberal handful of the big schoolships–together for the races, the STA has steadfastly held host ports to strict conditions regarding provision of services to ships and wholesome activities for crews and trainees, and has done its utmost to prevent commercialism from overshadowing the ideals of sail training during the in-port events of each race series.

Another result of the STA's phenomenal success, and a heartening validation of its ideals, has been the establishment of sail training associations in other countries. These retain strong ties to the STA, but tend to focus more broadly on coordinating and encouraging the development of sail training programs and less on the narrower role of organizing annual races. The first of such associations was the American Sail Training Association, or ASTA, established in 1973 and initially modeled quite closely on the STA, with the idea of organizing races among the relatively few sail training vessels then operating in U.S. waters. In the more than 20 years since its founding, however, ASTA–and sail training in the U.S.–have evolved in ways that reflect our own geographic and cultural characteristics, and respond to American needs. The same is, of course, true in the other countries where sail training has taken root.

Where sail training in the UK is generally understood to mean a seagoing voyage of a week or more in duration and involving young people between 15 and 25 who have little or no prior sailing experience, ASTA's member organizations include a wide range of programs involving cruises from a few hours to six weeks or more in length, "trainees" from elementary

"...less a training for *the sea than* through *the sea, and so benefit all walks of life..."*

Roger Archibald photo

school age to adults, and objectives ranging from pure adventure to serious scientific research. What ASTA members have in common is a shared belief that, no matter what other objectives may be served, putting people together on a sailing vessel and involving them in the work of sailing the ship can often be a life-changing experience. This belief is reflected in ASTA's stated mission, which very much embodies the traditional ideals of sail training: "to encourage character building through sail training, promote sail training to the American public, and support education under sail."

Recognizing the popularity of tall ships events and their enormous potential value in bringing to the American public a greater awareness of the ideals of sail training, ASTA has devoted increasing energy to organizing a series of Tall Ships Rallies each summer in conjunction with harbor or waterfront festivals. Originally conceived as an alternative to races, rallies involve crews in various forms of competition, both at sea and ashore, emphasizing seamanship, safety, and teamwork. In the process of developing this concept, ASTA has cultivated close relationships with port cities from the mid-Atlantic states to New England and the Great Lakes, and in 1993 held its first West Coast rally in San Francisco Bay. The effort to extend this idea to other regions, and thus stimulate public interest in and support for local sail training programs, will continue.

As the end of the twentieth century approaches, what is the future of sail training, both at home and around the world? On one hand, it seems doubtful that the fleet of big square-rigged schoolships will continue to expand; properly maintained, those now in existence will sail for many years to come, but whether they will be replaced when they come to the end of their useful lives seems unlikely. Some, after all–like the great Russian barques *Sedov* and *Kruzenshtern*– are more than 60 years old, and many, like the superb sister ships *Eagle, Sagres II,* and *Tovaritsch*, are nearly so. On the other hand, the number of relatively smaller vessels providing youth (and adult) sail training for adventure, education, and character development seems very likely to continue to grow: vessels like Australia's *Young Endeavour,* England's *Lord Nelson,* Japan's *Kaisei,* and the American *Corwith Cramer* and *Tole Mour,* as well as many others– not to mention the traditional, but smaller, schoolships like Poland's *Iskra* and Bulgaria's *Kaliakra*. All of these vessels are under 200 feet and were built within the last ten years; they serve a remarkable variety of "trainees": naval midshipmen, high school and college students, disadvantaged and adjudicated youth, disabled youth and adults. This, I believe, gives us a glimpse of the future of sail training: fewer big schoolships training professionals, but more and more smaller vessels providing a seagoing experience to a greater variety of people.

To celebrate the beginning of the new century, the STA is already planning a Transatlantic tall ships race–to be called "Tall Ships 2000®–that promises to be the largest-ever assemblage of sail training vessels. Following a course similar to that followed by the "Grand Regatta Columbus" in 1992, this magnificent fleet will originate in Europe and sail across the Atlantic to visit ports on the eastern seaboard of North America during the first summer of the new century; similar events are under consideration in the Pacific. Unlike such gatherings in 1976, 1986, and 1992, this fleet will not come to help celebrate a historic anniversary of past events; rather, it will bring the message of the energy and idealism of young people from around the world–the hope of the future. ASTA will be working closely with the STA and with U.S. port cities during the next few years to help plan events on this side of the Atlantic, and to insure that the message of sail training remains at the forefront–a message that seems more valid today than ever before. Training *for* the sea in big square-riggers may gradually disappear over the horizon, but training *through* the sea, in "tall ships" both large and small, can continue to help the nations of the world develop the leaders and citizens they will need to meet the challenges of the 21st century.

As operations officer aboard Eagle, *Captain Wood participated in the 1972 Cutty Sark Tall Ships Races; he returned to command* Eagle *in 1988, and was at the helm during the "Grand Regatta Columbus Quincentenary" in 1992. Retired from the Coast Guard, he now serves as a member of ASTA's Board of Directors and is U.S. National Representative to the STA's International Racing Committee.*

[1]Information on ships participating in the 1956 and 1964 Tall Ships Races was obtained from Hans Freiherr von Stackelberg's *Rahsegler im Rennen: Reisen und Regatten der "Gorch Fock"* published by Verlag Duburger Bücherzentrale, Flensburg, Germany, 1965. Captain von Stackelberg was an officer of *Gorch Fock* in 1964 and later commanded the ship during the 1970's.

[2]Quoted in *Outward Bound USA* by Joshua L. Miner and Joe Boldt, New York, William Morrow and Co., 1981.

[3]Information on British sail training programs, and on the history of the STA, is derived from John Hamilton's *Sail Training: The Message of the Tall Ships*, published by Patrick Stephens Ltd., Wellingborough, UK, 1988. John Hamilton was the STA Race Director from 1976 to 1992.

ASTA
MEMBER VESSELS
UNDERWAY...

A. J. MEERWALD

Rig gaff schooner. **Homeport/waters** Bivalve, N.J.: Delaware Bay and coastal New Jersey.

Who sails? School groups from elementary school (3rd grade) through high school, adult programs, and teacher workshops. Special education for middle and high school students, youth-at-risk, adjudicated youth. Affiliated with Rutgers University, Stockton State College and Rowan College.

The Delaware Bay Schooner Project has recently completed restoration of a remnant of the era when prosperity and harvesting the resources of the Delaware Bay went hand in hand. The 1928 oyster schooner, *A. J. Meerwald*, has been returned to her original glory as a representative of the heyday of the Delaware Estuary's productivity. She was one of the hundreds of Delaware Bay oyster schooners that participated in the region's multi-million dollar industry and is a product of a shipbuilding industry in South Jersey that served as a mainstay of the local economy.

While the vessel was being restored, on the banks of the Maurice River where she spent much of her career, educational programs related to the resources of Delaware Bay were offered to the general public and school groups. The schooner will sail her native waters carrying "deckloads" of people, providing access to the marine environment, education, and maritime heritage of the region and stressing the need for stewardship of the Bay's environment. As a land-based introduction to people sailing on the schooner an exhibit entitled "Maritime Traditions of the Delaware Bay" is housed at the Schooner Center in Port Norris.

Program Type Sail training for crew/apprentices, marine biology, environmental studies, maritime history, and dockside interpretation during home and port visits.

Specs Sparred length: 115'. LOA: 85'. LOD: 85'. LWL: 71'. Draft: 6'3". Beam: 22'1". Rig height: 75'. Freeboard: 2'. Sail area: 4,127 sq. ft. Tons: 57 grt. Power: diesel. Hull: wood. Designer: Traditional. Built: 1928; Charles H. Stowman and Sons Shipyard, Dorchester, NJ. **Coast Guard cert.** Passenger vessel (Subchapter T). **Sex** co-ed.

Contact Meghan Wren, Delaware Bay Schooner Project, PO Box 57, Dorchester; NJ 08316; 609 785-2060; FAX 609 785-2893.

ADIRONDACK

Rig schooner. **Homeport/waters** Newport, R.I./Fort Lauderdale, Fla.: Protected waters within 20 miles of harbor.

Who sails? School groups from elementary school through college, individuals and families.

The schooner *Adirondack* is the third of four schooners to come out of the Scarano Boat Building yard, beginning with the 59' schooner *Madeleine* in 1991, and continuing with the 105' schooner *America*, launched in July 1995. *Adirondack* combines the virtues of turn-of-the-century American schooner yachts with the latest in laminated wood technology. Offering an enviable combination of stability and speed, the *Adirondack* fulfills the builder and owner's ambition of providing a quality sailing experience to as many people as possible. Available to the public on a charter or two-hour excursion basis, the *Adirondack* pursues its mission to instill a love of sailing in each of her passengers and may be found in Newport, Rhode Island, during the summer season and Fort Lauderdale, Florida, for the winter season.

Program type Sail training with paying trainees. Passenger day sails.

Specs Sparred length: 80'. LOA: 65. LOD: 64'6". LWL: 58'. Draft: 8'. Beam: 16'. Rig height: 62'. Freeboard: 3'4". Sail area: 1,850 sq. ft. Tons: 41 grt. Power: twin 50 hp diesel. Hull: wood. **Coast Guard cert.** Passenger vessel (Subchapter T). **Crew** 3. Trainees: 49.

Contact Rick Scarano, Manager, Sailing Excursions, Inc., c/o Scarano Boat, Port Albany, Albany, NY 12202; 800 701-SAIL; 518 463-8401; 518 463-3407.

ADVENTURE

Rig schooner, 2-masted. **Homeport/waters** Gloucester, Mass.

Adventure is a "knockabout" schooner; designed without a bowsprit, she was safer at sea during sail changes than were schooners with bowsprits, which were known as "widowmakers." One of the best fishing schooners of her day, known as a "highliner," *Adventure* was the champion moneymaker of the fleet. She is the last of the Gloucester fishing schooners still in service under sail, and when she stopped fishing in 1953 her diesel engine was removed and *Adventure* began a second career as a windjammer off the Maine coast.

In 1988 *Adventure* was presented to the people and town of Gloucester, MA. Both at sea and at dockside, the vessel is now busy educating and entertaining the public. Restoration work is ongoing; much of the planking and many frames on the port side have been replaced, and plans have been made for continuing needed restoration in order to receive full re-certification by the Coast Guard. The Gloucester Adventure, Inc., invites you to step on board and to find out about the fishing heritage of New England as it was practiced at New England's busiest fishing port.

Program type Informal in-house programming in marine science, maritime history and ecology. Dockside interpretation.

Specs LOA: 121.5'. LOD: 121.5'. LWL: 109'. Draft: 13'6". Beam: 24'6". Rig height: 110'. Sail area: 6,500 sq. ft. Tons: 130 grt. Power: none. Hull: wood. Designer: Tom McManus. Built: 1926; John F. James & Son Yard, Essex, Mass.

Contact Marty Krugman, Gloucester Adventure, Inc., PO Box 1306, Gloucester, MA 01930; 508 281-8079; FAX 508 281-2393.

ADVENTURESS

Rig gaff topsail schooner, 2-masted. **Homeport/waters** Port Townsend, Wash.: Puget Sound, San Juan Islands, Port Townsend.

Who sails? School and other groups from elementary school through college, individuals and families. **Season** March to November. **Cost** $25-$45 per person for 3-5 hour sail. $65 per youth per day. $105 per person for adults. $1,600 per day for youth groups; $2,500 group rate for adults. Scholarships available.

Built for John Borden to gather Arctic specimens for a natural history museum, *Adventuress* sailed from Maine for the Bering Sea via the Straits of Magellan. From 1915 to 1952, she served the San Francisco Bar Pilots. She has sailed the waters of Puget Sound since 1959, and she is designated a National Historic Landmark.

Adventuress operates two distinct programs. Sound Exploration consists of two- to 10-day voyages in Puget Sound, the San Juan Islands and British Columbia. Programs emphasize non-competitive, hands-on learning to build self-confidence and develop a commitment to caring for each other and the environment. The programs are open to participants age 12 and older, as well as to Elderhostel, teacher training, women's and other groups. Sound Studies are half-day introductions to the marine ecology and history of Puget Sound. Approximately 100 three- and five-hour programs are offered each spring from as many as 20 town docks around Puget Sound. *Adventuress* meets or exceeds all U.S. Coast Guard applicable standards and is always under the command of a licensed captain.

Program type Marine science, maritime history and ecology. Passenger day and overnight sails. Dockside interpretation during port visits.

Specs Sparred length: 135'. LOA: 102'. LWL: 71'. Draft: 12'. Beam: 21'. Rig height: 110'. Sail area: 5,478 sq. ft. Sail no.: TS 15. Tons: 82 grt. Power: 250 hp, diesel. Hull: wood. Designer: B. B. Crowninshield. Built: 1913; Rice Brothers, East Boothbay, Me. **Coast Guard cert.** Passenger vessel (Subchapter T). **Crew** 4-5; 8-10 instructors. Trainees: 45 day; 25 overnight. Age: 8-adult. Sex: co-ed.

Contact Jenell DeMatteo, Executive Director, Sound Experience, 2730 Washington St., #D, Port Townsend, WA 98368; 360 379-0438.

ALASKA EAGLE

Former name *Flyer*. **Rig** sloop. **Homeport/waters** Newport Beach, Calif.: South Pacific, New Zealand.

Who sails? Individual college students and adults. **Cost** $130 per person per day.

Winner of the 1977-78 Whitbread Round the World Race as the Dutch yacht *Flyer*, the 65-foot *Alaska Eagle* now operates as a sail-training vessel for adults and college students interested in acquiring offshore passage-making skills. Since 1982, *Alaska Eagle* has made more than 22 Pacific crossings and sailed more than 130,000 miles with students aboard. Cruises and passages are generally two to three weeks in length.

Strong and fast, *Alaska Eagle* is a comfortable offshore cruiser with four private staterooms and two heads and showers. Under the guidance of two USCG-licensed skipper/instructors, *Alaska Eagle's* nine-member crews participate in all aspects of vessel management at sea: watch standing, sail handling, steering and navigating. A professional cook handles the meals. *Alaska Eagle* is operated by the Sailing Center at Orange Coast College, a Southern California non-profit boating education program.

Plans for 1997 include:
- Wellington, New Zealand to Papeete, Tahiti - March 30 to April 19, 1997.
- Papeete, Tahiti to Honolulu, HI - April 22 to May 11, 1997.
- Honolulu, HI to Newport Beach, CA - May 14 to May 30, 1997.

Program type Sail training with paying trainees. Paying passengers on overnight passages.

Specs Sparred length: 65'. LOA: 65'. LOD: 65'. LWL: 50'. Draft: 10'5". Beam: 16'4". Rig height: 90'. Freeboard: 5'. Sail area: 1,500 sq. ft. Tons: 39 grt. Power: 200 hp diesel. Hull: aluminum. Designer: Sparkman & Stephens. Built: 1977, Royal Nuisman Shipyard, Holland. **Coast Guard cert**. Sailing school vessel (Subchapter R). **Crew** 3. **Trainees**: 9.

Contact Kim Miller, Adventure Sailing Coordinator, Orange Coast College Sailing Center, 1801 West Coast Highway, Newport Beach, CA 92663; 714 645-9412; FAX 714 645-1859.

ALERT OF CUTTYHUNK

Rig staysail schooner. **Homeport/waters** Greenwich, CT: New York to Cape Cod.

Who sails? School groups from elementary school through college, individuals, and families.

The 64'5" *"Alert" of
Cuttyhunk* was built in 1917 for
Captain "Billy" Raymond by the
C.A. Anderson Boatyard in
Wareham, Massachusetts.
Captain Billy had been hired to
transport building materials for
William M. Wood, who planned
to build a large summer home
on Cuttyhunk Island. The *Alert*
continued to supply Cuttyhunk
Island with Mail Service, supplies, and year-round passenger
ferry service through 1987. In
1991, after years of neglect, the
historic vessel was purchased
from the state of Massachusetts
by Carl Piemental and
relaunched. She was sold in 1995
to Bob Rosenbaum, an avid ship
stamp collector and boat design-
er/builder, formally of

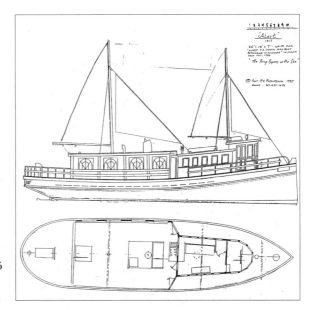

Sparkman & Stephens and Holland Marine Design. He undertook the project to restore *Alert*
to her former glory. Captain Rosenbaum plans to make *Alert* available to the public once
again offering a variety of educational programs as well as historic waterfront tours. In keeping with *Alert's* historic past, Captain Rosenbaum has plans to bid for the Mail Service contract
to Cuttyhunk Island in 1999. The vessel is also available for private charter.

Program Type Sail training with paying trainees, marine science, maritime history, and seamanship. Passenger day sails and dockside interpretation during port visits.

Specs Sparred length: 65'. LOA: 65'. LOD: 65'. LWL: 58'. Draft: 7'. Beam: 18'. Rig
height: 41'. Freeboard: 6'. Tons: 49 grt. Power: 6M-6-110 diesel. Hull: wood. Designer:
C. A. Anderson. Built: 1917; C. A. Anderson, Wareham, MA. **Coast Guard cert.** Passenger
vessel (Subchapter T). **Crew** 2. Trainees: 48.

Contact Captain Bob Rosenbaum, Greenwich Yacht Charter, P. O. Box 1544, Greenwich, CT
06830; 203 358-2695.

ALEXANDRIA

Former names *Lindø, Yngve.* **Rig** square topsail schooner, 3-masted. **Homeport/waters** Alexandria, Va.: Atlantic Ocean and Gulf of Mexico.

Who sails? Elementary, high school and adult education groups, individuals and families. Court referrals for some activities. **Season** April to November.

The schooner *Alexandria* is a living landmark that recalls the heyday and prosperity of a by-gone shipping industry in the City of Alexandria and on the Potomac River and Chesapeake Bay. Originally built as a merchant ship in Sweden, today *Alexandria* provides programs and activities for the pleasure and education of the public. *Alexandria*'s volunteers maintain the historic wooden vessel while at the same time provide a full sailing season and educational program. In recent years the ship has visited maritime centers and waterfront festivals between New Orleans and Boston, and appeared in the movie *Interview with a Vampire.*

The *Alexandria* offers an extensive program of community-based programs ranging from the Sea Cadet programs to sail training classes in accordance with ASTA guidelines, from operating as a Halloween haunted ship to being available for dockside receptions, parties, and specialty events. Sea Cadets pursue a hands-on training program. Adult crew are encouraged to work towards receiving or upgrading Coast Guard licenses, beginning with Level 1, Apprentice Seamen, to Bosun and higher.

Program type Sail training for crew/apprentices and with paying trainees. Sea education in cooperation with accredited schools and other organized groups such as Scouts. Passenger day and overnight sails. Dockside interpretation.

Specs Sparred length: 125'. LOA: 92'. LOD: 92'. LWL: 92'. Draft: 10'. Beam: 26'. Rig height: 100'. Sail area: 7,800 sq. ft. Sail no.: 13. Tons: 76 grt. Power: 250 hp Volvo-Penta diesel. Hull: wood. Designer: Albert Svensson & Karl Ogard. Built: 1929; Albert Svensson. **Coast Guard cert**. Attraction vessel. **Crew** 6-12 (day); 10-15 (overnight). Trainees: 6. Age: all. Sex: co-ed. Dockside visitors: 90.

Contact Stanley Martin, President, Alexandria Seaport Foundation, 1000 South Lee St., Jones Point, Alexandria, VA 22314; 703 549-7078; FAX 703 549-6715. E-mail: ASFHQS@aol.com.

ALMA

Rig scow schooner, 2-masted. **Homeport/waters** San Francisco: San Francisco Bay.

Who sails? Adult education groups, individual students and adults, families.

The scow schooner *Alma* was built at Hunters Point in San Francisco Bay in 1891 and is the last of approximately 400 scow schooners that carried cargo all across the San Francisco Bay area at the turn of the century. She is owned and operated by the National Park Service San Francisco Maritime National Historical Park in San Francisco and docked at Hyde Street Pier near Fisherman's Wharf. The National Maritime Museum Association supports operations of the *Alma* at the many maritime festivals and parades in the Bay area.

Alma sails from March until November and is crewed by volunteers that participate in a "sweat equity" program that helps maintain all the historic vessels at Hyde Street Pier. *Alma* represents and interprets a time before bridges and paved roads, when commerce moved by boat around the Bay. The *Alma* volunteer program enables trainees and apprentices to learn about traditional sailing and wooden boat maintenance. No fees are required as all crew volunteer to sail and maintain the *Alma* and other park vessels.

Program type Sail training for crew and apprentices. Sea education based on informal in-house programs focuses on maritime history. Dockside interpretation. Affiliated groups include the National Maritime Museum Association, San Francisco National Maritime Historical Park and National Park Service.

Specs Sparred length: 88'. LOA: 62'. LOD: 61'4". LWL: 59'5". Draft: 3'6". Beam: 23'6". Rig height: 76'. Freeboard: 4'. Sail area: 2,684 sq. ft. Tons: 47 grt. Power: (2) 671 GMC diesels. Hull: wood. Designer: Fred Siemers. Built: 1891; Fred Siemers, San Francisco. **Crew** 6. Trainees: 28 (overnight); 40 (day). Age: 14+.

Contact William G. Thomas, Superintendent, San Francisco Maritime National Historical Park, Building E, Fort Mason Center, San Francisco, CA 94123; 415 556-1659; FAX 415 556-6293.

AMERICA

Rig gaff schooner, 2-masted. **Homeport/waters** Annapolis, MD: Mid-Atlantic, New England, Florida, Caribbean and the Mediterranean.

Named for the famed New York-built yacht that crossed the Atlantic to win the £100 Cup in 1851, and then gave her name to the world's most coveted yachting trophy, *America* was built to demonstrate American excellence in technology, craftsmanship, and ingenuity in every port she visits worldwide. While *America* is a waterline up re-creation of the 1851 yacht, her spars utilize the latest in carbon fiber technology, and *America* will weigh some 50 tons less than the original George Steers-designed schooner. Below decks she will benefit from the most advanced boat building technologies available, showcasing goods and service from, among others, US Paint Corp., 3M's Marine Division, Harken, Hood Sails, ZF Industries and Marine Air. With plans to sail an average of 20,000 miles per year, *America* will visit all major "in-water" boat shows, classic yacht regattas, OpSail 2000 in New York Harbor, the 2001 Sesquicentennial of the Royal Yacht Squadron Regatta of 1851 in Cowes, and other events.

Program type Sail training for crew apprentices. Sea education based on informal in-house programming. Passenger day and overnight sails. Dockside interpretation during port visits.

Specs Sparred length: 139'. LOA: 105'. LOD: 105'. LWL: 90'6". Draft: 10'. Beam: 25'. Rig height: 108'. Freeboard: 4'. Sail area: 6,400 sq. ft. Tons: 120 grt. Power: 2 John Deere. Designer: George Steers, w/modifications by Scarano Boat. Built: 1995; Scarano Boat, Port Albany, N.Y. **Coast Guard cert**. Passenger vessel (Subchapter T). Sex: co-ed.

Contact Kendra Houghton, Director of Public Relations, Schooner America USA, Inc., 100 North Union St., Alexandria, VA 22314; 703 683-4654; FAX 703 683-1411.

AMERICAN ROVER

Rig topsail schooner, 3-masted. **Homeport/waters** Norfolk, Va.: Chesapeake Bay & tributaries.

Who sails? Individuals, families, and student groups. Affiliated institutions include Old Dominion University. **Cost** $12-$16 per person, 2-3 hours; $9-$13 per person group rate, 2-3 hours.

The *American Rover* operates a rigorous day sailing schedule out of the Norfolk, Virginia, waterfront. Cruises are generally 2-to-3 hour sightseeing and historical tours. Special student educational field trips are also popular.

Program type Sail training for crew and apprentices. Sea education in marine science, maritime history and ecology in cooperation with schools and colleges. Day sails. Homeport dockside interpretation. Clientele includes students from elementary school through college, as well as adults and families.

Specs Sparred length: 135'. LOA: 98'. LOD: 96'. LWL: 80'. Draft: 8.5'. Beam: 24'. Rig height: 85'. Freeboard: 8'. Sail area: 5,000 sq. ft. Tons: 98 grt. Power: 240 hp. Designer: Merritt Walter. Built: 1986; Kolsar & Rover Marine, Panama City, Fla. **Coast Guard cert.** Passenger vessel (Subchapter T). **Crew:** 4. Non-crew educators 2. Trainees: 149 (max.). Sex: co-ed. Dockside visitors: 149.

Contact Captain Brook J. Smith, Master, Rover Marine, Inc., PO Box 3125, Norfolk, VA 23514; 804 627-7245; FAX 804 627-6626.

ANGELIQUE

Rig gaff topsail ketch. **Homeport/waters** Camden, Me.: coastal New England.

Who sails? Individuals and groups aged 15 and up. Affiliated institutions include the College of the Atlantic. **Season** May to October.

The gaff topsail ketch *Angelique* was designed especially for the New England windjammer trade. Built in 1980, her design mirrors the swift, powerful and seaworthy 19th-century vessels of the North Sea and English Channel. *Angelique* meets Coast Guard specifications for sailing vessels carrying passengers. She has a professional crew of seven, and accommodations for 31 guests or participants. *Angelique* is available for 3-, 4- and 6-day traditional windjammer cruises as well as group or corporate charters. On her cruises *Angelique* makes her way to such favorite spots as Mt. Desert, Isle au Haut and Swans Island. *Angelique*'s tanbark sails are a familiar sight along the rugged Maine coats.

Program type Windjammer vacations, Elderhostel, maritime history, environmental studies, and sail training.

Specs Sparred length: 130'. LOD: 95'. LWL: 83'. Draft: 11'. Beam: 24'. Rig height: 100'. Sail area: 5,300 sq. ft. Tons: 142 grt. Power: 300 hp diesel. Hull: steel. Designer: Imero Gobatto. Built: 1980; Putnam Shipyard. **Coast Guard cert**. Passenger vessel (Subchapter T). **Crew** 6. Trainees: 85 (day); 31 (overnight). Age: 15. Sex: co-ed.

Contact Captain Mike and Lynne McHenry, Yankee Packet Co., PO Box 736, Camden, ME 04843; 207 236-8873; FAX 207 785-6036. E-mail: sailypc@midcoast.com.

APPLEDORE II

Rig gaff topsail schooner, 2-masted. **Homeport/waters** Camden, Me.: Maine to the Florida Keys. **Season** June to October (Maine); December to May (Florida).

Who sails? School groups from elementary school through college, individuals and families.

The *Appledore* is a traditional gaff-rigged schooner designed for ocean sailing. Launched in 1978 at the Gamage Ship Yard in South Bristol, Maine, Bud McIntosh circumnavigated the world on her maiden voyage, an adventure documented in Herbert Smith's, *Dreams of Natural Places* and *Sailing Three Oceans*. Homeported in Camden, Maine, where she makes day sails from late June until mid-October, *Appledore II* sails out of Key West, Florida during the winter months, where she undertakes snorkel trips on North America's only living coral reef, as well as sunset cruises. She carries up to 49 passengers on day sails and can accommodate up to 26 overnight.

The crew of the *Appledore* is committed to sail training, and they are trained in sailing, celestial navigation, and marlinespike seamanship through operation of the vessel on day sails as well as two 2,000-mile offshore voyages yearly. Interested persons are encouraged to contact us for possible payroll or volunteer positions. We have opportunities for not only crew, but business positions on an entry level.

Program type Sail training for crew and apprentices. Sea education based on informal in-house programming. Passenger day sails. Dockside interpretation.

Specs Sparred length: 86'. LOA: 82'. LOD: 65'. LWL: 53'. Draft: 10'6". Beam: 18'9" Rig height: 90'. Freeboard: 7'. Sail area: 2,815 sq. ft. Tons: 63 grt. Power: Cummins 210 diesel. Hull: wood. Designer: Bud McIntosh. Built: 1978; Gamage Shipyard, South Bristol, Me. **Coast Guard cert**. Passenger vessel (Subchapter T). **Crew** 7. Trainees: 49 (day); 20 (overnight). Age: 21-40. Sex: co-ed. Dockside visitors: 52.

Contact John P. McKean, President, Schooner Exploration Associates, Ltd., "0" Lily Pond Dr., Camden, ME 04843; 207 236-8353, 800 233-PIER (summer); PO Box 4114, Key West, FL 33041-4114; 305 296-9992 (winter).

ARGUS

Rig topsail ketch. **Homeport/waters** Newport Beach Calif.: Catalina Island, Long Beach Harbor, Dana Point.

Who sails? Boy Scouts operate the vessel as crew/trainees under the tutelage of ship's captains and crew trainers.. **Season** year round. **Cost** Variable; 1-day, weekend, week-long - inquire Sea Base Director.

Laid down and launched as a merchant vessel for work in the Baltic and Scandinavian waters, *Argus* probably began life as a salt fish carrier, but later carried a variety of cargoes including grain. In 1968 she was sailed from the Baltic to Spain, Canary Islands, then across the Atlantic to the Caribbean, through the Panama Canal, and north to Newport Beach, California. She has been used, abused, and loved by Sea Scouts ever since, has a large diesel engine, has a full component of working sails, which include three jibs, main, mizzen, and main topsail and course. She is supported by the "Friends of Argus," who enlist and train crew members, and the Orange County Council of the BSA, who bear the burden of financial support and arranging Sea Scout high adventure sails. *Argus* takes five-day and two-day trips at sea to Catalina Island and coastal ports for a working sail training cruise with trainees climbing the rigging, helmsmanship, small boat handling, snorkeling, swimming, beach hikes, and the experience of night watches.

Program type Sail training and sea education.

Specs Sparred length: 92'. LOA: 68'. LOD: 65'. Draft: 8'. Beam: 18'. Rig height: 60'. Freeboard: 4'6". Sail area: 2,510 sq. ft. Tons: 53 grt. Power: Detroit 671 diesel. Hull: wood. Built: 1905; Marstal, Denmark. **Coast Guard cert**. Passenger vessel (Subchapter T). **Crew** 6. Trainees: 34 (day); 20 (overnight).

Contact William Mountford, Sea Base Manager, Boy Scout Sea Base, 1931 West Pacific Coast Highway, Newport Beach, CA 92663; 714 642-5031; FAX 714 650-5407.

BEE, HMS

Rig gaff schooner, 2-masted. **Homeport/waters** Penetanguishene, Ont.: Georgian Bay and Lake Huron.

Who sails? Individuals and groups. **Season** June to September. **Cost** Can $20 per person per three-hour sail.

H. M. Schooner *Bee* is a replica of the transport schooner/ gunboat *Bee*, which sailed out of the Royal Navy Establishment at Penetanguishene in the early 1800s. With its emphasis on living history, a sail on the *Bee* takes you back to the days of wooden ships and iron men. Discovery Harbour at Penetanguishene on Georgian Bay oper- ates land and sailing programs for the public. Costumed

interpreters bring the history and activities of the site to life with everything from musketry demonstrations to sailing programs. Constructed at the Establishment and launched in 1984, *Bee* is one of a growing fleet of vessels at this outpost of the Royal Navy. She operates from June to September on the waters of Georgian Bay. Sail training adventures consist of three-hour trips during which participants become part of the crew and learn to hoist sails, sweat halyards, and take part in all operations of a Royal Navy vessel.

Program type Seamanship.

Specs Sparred length: 78'. LOA: 48'6". LWL: 42'. Draft: 5'6". Beam: 14'6". Sail area: 1,672 sq. ft. Tons: 25 grt. Power: 90 hp diesel. Hull: GRP and wood. Designer: Steve Killing. Built: 1985; Charlie Allen, Penetanguishene, Ont. **Crew** 7. Trainees: 14. Age: 10+.

Contact Chris Bagley, Marine Coordinator, Discovery Harbour/Havre de la Découverte, Penetanguishene, Ontario; 705 549-8064; FAX 705 549-4858.

BILL OF RIGHTS

Rig gaff topsail schooner, 2-masted. **Homeport/waters** Philadelphia, Pa.: Atlantic Ocean and Gulf of Mexico (Eastport, Me., to Brownsville, Tex.).

Who sails? Participation is by reference from a cooperating agency. **Season** year round.

The *Bill of Rights* is one of two ships operated by VisionQuest, a non-profit organization that offers alternatives to conventional incarceration for troubled youths. Through VisionQuest's OceanQuest program, trainees spend up to eight months at sea, learning the basic tenets of sailing while also receiving daily schooling and regular counseling. The challenges of life on board a sailing ship, combined with the guidance of VisionQuest's professional treatment staff, help them recognize and overcome personal issues. The *Bill of Rights* spends its winters in Florida and summers in Maine. The ship's crew of 19 VisionQuest youths, 10 treatment staff and three maritime staff, spend five days a week at sea.

The OceanQuest program has proven very effective in instilling a sense of self-discipline and respect for authority while developing skilled crews. In 1992, VisionQuest's OceanQuest program was recognized by ASTA as the Sail Training Program of the Year. A replica of an 1856 gaff topsail schooner, she sailed from Newport, Rhode Island, for 17 years as a charter vessel before being purchased by VisionQuest in 1987.

Program type Sail training for crew and apprentices. Trainees are chosen by private placement or court referral.

Specs Sparred length: 136'. LOA: 129'. LOD: 94'. LWL: 85'. Draft: 10'. Beam: 23'. Rig height: 100'. Freeboard: 5'8". Sail area: 6,300 sq. ft. Sail no.: 3. Tons: 95. Power: Caterpillar diesel 210 hp. Hull: wood. Designer: McCurdy, Rhodes & Bates. Built: 1971; Harvey F. Gamage, South Bristol, Me. **Coast Guard cert**. Passenger vessel (Subchapter T). **Crew** 5 (day); 8 (overnight); 5 instructors. Trainees: 52 (day sails); 39 (overnight).

Contact Maragret Lannon, Program Master, VisionQuest National, Ltd., PO Box 447, Exton, PA 19341; 602 881-3950.

BLACK JACK

Rig brigantine. **Homeport/waters** Ottawa, Ontario: Ottawa River

Who sails? High schools and colleges as well as individuals of student age. **Season** April to October. **Cost** Inquire.

Built in 1952 by the late Captain Thomas G. Fuller, *Black Jack* is an 87' brigantine built of steel. Carrying 3,000 square feet of sail, the ship is now used as a sail training vessel plying the Ottawa River in Canada as well as the Great Lakes and eastern seaboard under the flag of Bytown Brigantine. Carrying a crew of 12 trainees plus crew, the vessel has become an icon in Ottawa, Canada's capital city, with its devotion to historical accuracy and traditional sailing. Thomas Fuller was one of Canada's most decorated war heroes, earning the name "Pirate of the Adriatic" and holding the distinction of the longest time served in offensive war action. His wartime experience taught him the value of instilling confidence and resourcefulness in our youth through adventure at sea. Thomas Fuller founded Bytown Brigantine, Inc., a non-profit organization, in 1984 to provide traditional sail training to local youths.

Program type Sail training with paying trainees. Sea education in maritime history in cooperation with other organized groups such as Scouts. Dockside interpretation during outport visits.

Specs Sparred length: 95'. LOA: 87'. LOD: 68". LWL: 57'. Draft: 6'. Beam: 15'. Rig height: 80'. Freeboard: 3'. Sail area: 3,000 sq. ft. Tons: 42.25 grt. Power: GM 671. Hull: steel. Designer: Thomas G. Fuller. Built: 1952; Thomas G. Fuller, Ottawa, Ont. **Crew** 18 (5 Canadian Merchant Marine officers, 1 cook and 12 deckhands). Trainees: 80 (day). Sex: co-ed.

Contact Simon A. F. Fuller, President, Bytown Brigantine, Inc., 2700 Queensview Dr., Ottawa, Ontario K2B 8H6 Canada; 613 820-6000; FAX 613 596-5947.

BLACK PEARL

Rig brigantine. **Homeport/waters** Bridgeport, N.Y.: Atlantic Ocean and Caribbean Sea.

Who sails? School and other groups and individuals. Affiliated groups include Univ. of Bridgeport, Housatonic Community College and seven Connecticut school districts. **Season** May to October.

Built in 1938 by Lincoln Vaughan for his own use, *Black Pearl* was purchased by Barclay H. Warburton III in 1958. Long a believer in the sea as a teacher, Warburton selected the rig as a good one for sail training. In 1972, Warburton sailed the *Black Pearl* to England to participate in the Tall Ship Race in European waters, becoming the first American to do so. On his return to Newport, Warburton founded the American Sail Training Association.

Black Pearl is currently owned by the "H.M.S." Rose Foundation and operated by the Aquaculture Foundation, a non-profit corporation formed to promote quality education in marine studies. Her programs take her throughout Long Island Sound, as well as into the North Atlantic, Gulf of Mexico and Caribbean.

Program type Sail training for crew and paying trainees. Sea education in marine science, maritime history and ecology in cooperation with accredited schools and colleges. Passenger day sails and overnight

Specs Sparred length: 79'. LOD: 52'. LWL: 43'. Draft: 9'. Beam: 14'. Rig height: 63'. Freeboard: 6'. Sail area: 2,000 sq. ft. Sail no.: TS US-33. Tons: 28 grt. Power: diesel. Designer: Edson Schock. Built: 1938; C. Lincoln Vaughan, Wickford, R.I. **Crew** 3-4 (day); 4-8 (overnight). Trainees: 6. Age: 14-65. Sex: co-ed. Dockside visitors: 15.

Contact Michael Williams, The Aquaculture Foundation, 45 Sherman St., Fairfield, CT 06430; 203 878-0662; FAX 203 878-9568; E-mail: MPAW@gnn.com.

BLUENOSE II

Rig gaff topsail schooner, 2-masted. **Homeport/waters** Lunenburg, Nova Scotia: East Coast Canada and United States.

Who sails? Individuals and groups. Affiliate institutions include the Fisheries Museum of the Atlantic, Lunenburg; Maritime Museum of the Atlantic, Halifax; Nova Scotia Nautical Institute, Port Hawkesbury, Canadian Forces (Navy) Halifax. **Season** April to October. **Cost** Adults Can $20; Seniors (over 65) Can $15; Children (under 12) Can $10.

The original schooner *Bluenose*, built in 1921, was a typical Nova Scotian Grand Banks fishing schooner. Built both for fishing and for the International Fishermen's Races between Canada and the USA, under Captain Angus Walters, *Bluenose* won the cup for Canada several times, and her likeness became a national emblem, depicted on stamps and coins. Launched on July 24, 1963, *Bluenose II* was built from *Bluenose*'s plans and by the same yard. The only difference lies in the accommodations for the 18-member crew, and the modern navigation and communication instruments. She serves as a goodwill ambassador for the Province of Nova Scotia, participating in tall ships events throughout the Western Hemisphere. *Bluenose II*'s contribution to sail training is mainly through the seamen and cadets who serve as part of the crew, receiving instructions from the officers as they work. Today she sails in the best *Bluenose* tradition under Captain Wayne A. S. Walters, Master Mariner, grandson of the legendary Angus.

Program type Sail training for crew and apprentices. Passenger day sails. Dockside interpretation.

Specs Sparred length: 181'. LOD: 143'. LWL: 112'. Draft: 16'. Beam: 27'. Rig height: 132'. Freeboard: 10'. Sail area: 11,696 sq. ft. Tons: 285 grt. Power: twin Caterpillar diesels. Hull: wood. Designer: William J. Roué. Built: 1963; Smith & Rhuland, Ltd. Lunenburg, Nova Scotia. **Coast Guard cert**. Canadian Coast guard certification. **Crew**: 18. Sex: co-ed. Dockside visitors: 200.

Contact Wilfred P. Moore, Chairman, Bluenose II Preservation Trust, PO Box 1963, Lunenburg, Nova Scotia B0J 2C0 Canada; 902 634-1963; FAX 902 634-1995.

BOUNTY, HMS

Rig full-rigged ship, 3-masted. **Homeport/waters** Fall River, Mass./St. Petersburg, Fla.: Atlantic Ocean and Gulf of Mexico.

The *Bounty* was built by MGM Studios to be used in filming the movie *Mutiny on the Bounty* in Tahiti. Following visits to England and New York, the *Bounty* became a popular tourist attraction in St. Petersburg, Florida. In 1986, the *Bounty* was purchased by Turner Broadcasting System, Inc., refitted, and once again put to sea. She participated in Operation Sail '86/Salute to Liberty, toured the East and West coasts, the Great Lakes, and was used in several movies.

In 1993, Turner Broadcasting System donated the *Bounty* to the Fall River Area Chamber of Foundation, Inc., and she is operated by the Tall Ship Bounty Foundation, Inc., with a mission to provide specialized support to the community, the state and the nation in the fields of education, environmental research, historic preservation, and business development. Emerging programs are being developed to utilize the *Bounty* to deliver an environmental message encouraging low-impact boating and a course for leadership training, teambuilding and confidence development for highly motivated youth.

Program type Sail training with crew and apprentices. Sea education in maritime history based on in-house programming. Dockside interpretation.

Specs Sparred length: 169'. LOA: 130'. LOD: 120'. Draft: 13'. Beam: 30'. Rig height: 115'. Freeboard: 12'. Sail area: 10,000 sq. ft. Tons: 412 grt. Power: twin 200 hp Caterpillar diesels. Hull: wood. Built: 1960; Smith & Rhuland, Lunenburg, Nova Scotia. **Coast Guard cert**. Uninspected yacht and attraction vessel. **Crew** 20 (day); 25 (overnight). Trainees: 100 (day). Dockside visitors: 150.

Contact Thomas P. Murray, Executive Director, Tall Ship Bounty Foundation, Inc., PO Box 990, Fall River, MA 02722; 508 673-3886; FAX 508 679-6178.

BOWDOIN

Rig Grand Banks knockabout schooner, 2-masted. **Homeport/waters** Castine, Me.: Gulf of Maine, Canadian Maritimes, western Greenland and Arctic.

Who sails? School groups from elementary school through college as well as individuals of all ages. Affiliated institutions include the Maine Maritime Academy. **Season** May to October. **Cost** $100 per person per day; $3,000 group rate.

The schooner *Bowdoin* is the flagship of Maine Maritime Academy's sail training fleet, and the official sailing vessel of the state of Maine. Built in 1921 specifically for cruising in Arctic waters, she is one of the strongest wooden vessels ever constructed. Between 1921 and 1954 she made 26 voyages to the far north under the command of her first master, explorer Donald B. MacMillan.

Today, with the characteristic ice barrel on her foremast, *Bowdoin* serves the students of the Maine Maritime Academy and the educational community of New England with a broad range of programs in seamanship, ocean studies and curriculum development. Offerings begin at the high school level, and range from cruises on Penobscot Bay to extended passages to the vessel's traditional cruising grounds of Greenland and Labrador. The latter occur semi-annually, and represent a unique opportunity in the world of sail training.

Program type Sail training with paying trainees. Sea education with organized groups with informal in-house programming in marine science and maritime history. Passenger day sails. Dockside interpretation at outports.

Specs Sparred length: 100'. LOA: 88'. LOD: 83'. LWL: 73'. Draft: 10'. Beam: 22'. Rig height: 70'. Freeboard: 4'. Sail area: 2,900 sq. ft. Tons: 66 grt. Power: 190 hp Cummins diesel. Hull: wood. Designer: William Hand. Built: 1921; Hodgdon Brothers Shipyard, East Boothbay, Me. **Coast Guard cert.** Sailing school vessel (Subchapter R) and Passenger vessel (Subchapter T). **Crew** 5; 1 instructor. Trainees: 44 (day); 11 (overnight). Age: 16+. Sex: co-ed.

Contact Linda Griffith, Bowdoin Coordinator, Maine Maritime Academy, Castine, ME 04420; 207 326-4311; FAX 207 326-2377.

BRILLIANT

Rig gaff schooner, 2-masted. **Homeport/waters** Mystic, Conn.: New England, Nova Scotia, Chesapeake Bay.

Who sails? High school and adult education programs and individuals of all ages. Affiliated institutions include Mystic Seaport Museum. **Season** spring to fall. **Cost** $125 per person per day; $110 per person (group rate).

One of the finest sailing vessels ever built and a veteran of several Bermuda races and transatlantic voyages, *Brilliant* was donated to Mystic Seaport in 1953. Today she provides a sea-going learning experience in which teenagers or adults can enjoy the adventure of saltwater cruising plus the practical applications of safety, seamanship and navigation. Aboard the *Brilliant,* the participants are the crew. Under the direction of the captain and the mate, the crew performs the ship's work, including steering, sail handling, cooking and cleaning.

The *Brilliant* program offers spring and fall cruises for adults with cruises for teens during the summer. Programs include weekend cruises from Friday through Monday, and six-day cruises running from Sunday through Friday. Longer cruises of up to 14 days are also scheduled. The *Brilliant* program is open to individuals and organized groups of adults or teenagers, male and female. Youth groups consist of one adult leader and nine teens. No previous experience is required for the coastwise cruises; ocean passages require some experience. All participants must be competent swimmers.

Program type Sail training with paying trainees. Sea education in cooperation with organized groups such as Scouts, based on informal in-house programming.

Specs Sparred length: 74'. LOA: 61'6". LOD: 61'6". LWL: 49'. Draft: 9'. Beam: 14'8'. Rig height: 81'. Tons: 30 grt. Power: 97 hp GMC diesel. Hull: wood. Designer: Sparkman & Stephens. Built: 1932; Henry B. Nevins, City Island, N.Y. **Coast Guard cert**. Sailing school vessel (Subchapter R) and passenger vessel (Subchapter T). **Crew** 3 (day); 4 (overnight). Trainees: 9-10 (day); 6 (overnight). Age: 15-19 (teen program); 20+ (adult program). Dockside visitors: 14.

Contact George H. Moffett, Museum Education Department, Mystic Seaport Museum, Box 6000, Mystic, CT 06355-0990; 860 572-0711; FAX 860 572-5328.

CALIFORNIAN

Rig square topsail schooner, 2-masted. **Homeport/waters** Coastal California and Pacific Ocean.

Who sails? School groups and individuals. **Season** year round. **Cost** $495 per student for 5-day Cadet voyage. $38 per student for Sea Chest program. $140 per person per day for adult programs.

Owned and operated by the not-for-profit Nautical Heritage Society, the *Californian* is a re-creation of the 1849 *Campbell*-class Revenue Marine Cutter, *C. W. Lawrence*. *Californian*'s sail training programs immerse trainees in a unique and valuable form of education that enables them to experience the forces of nature and develop skills that relate directly to life ashore. Self-reliance, teamwork, American history and coastal ecology as well as sailing are the corner-stones of the *Californian* programs. The Sea Chest Program provides curriculum materials for classroom use, ship tours and day sails for elementary school students. High school students can receive academic credit for time spent aboard, and college level programs are also available.

The ship has been designated as the Official Tallship Ambassador for the state of California. In addition to its ordinary coastwise sail training programs, the *Californian* has sailed to Hawaii, Canada, and took an extraordinary relief mission to offer humanitarian aid to Mexico when that country was devastated by the 1986 earthquake.

Program type Marine biology, maritime history, full curriculum academics, special education and environmental studies for middle school through adult.

Specs Sparred length: 145'. LOD: 93'5". Draft: 9'5". Beam: 24'6". Rig height: 101'. Freeboard: 6'. Sail area: 7,000 sq. ft. Tons: 98 grt. Power: 100 hp Caterpillar diesel. Hull: wood. Designer: Melbourne Smith. Built: 1983; Nautical Heritage Society, San Diego, Calif. **Coast Guard cert.** Passenger vessel (Subchapter T). **Crew** 8. Trainees: 16 (overnight). Age: 4th grade through college. Sex: co-ed.

Contact Steve Christman, President, Nautical Heritage Society, 24532 Del Prado, Dana Point, CA 92629; 714 661-1001; FAX 714-240-7842.

CHALLENGE

Rig staysail schooner, 3-masted. **Homeport/waters** Toronto, Ontario: Toronto Harbour, Lake Ontario.

Who sails? Individuals and groups of all ages. Affiliated institutions include the Canadian Sail Training Association, the Toronto Harbourfront Centre and the Marine Museum of Upper Canada. **Season** April to October. **Cost** Training cruise, Can $10 per trainee; 2-hour sail, Can $15.95 (adult), Can $9.95 (child); 4-hour charter: Can $1,750.

Challenge is a 96-foot three-masted staysail schooner. Built in Port Stanley, Ontario, in 1980, four years later she was lengthened and rebuilt for charter. Her heavy steel construction and modern rig combine for safe and swift passages. *Challenge* is also powered by an auxiliary Volvo diesel, which enables her to maintain a planned itinerary. *Challenge* meets all Canadian Coast Guard requirements for safety equipment and is insured to the highest degree. She carries two life rafts for 20 people each, a life platform for 69 passengers, and the most up-to-date fire detection, prevention and extinguishing equipment. She is certified to carry 75 day and 65 evening passengers. The ship is operated by a skilled crew of six professional sailors. *Challenge* is the perfect sail training ship - large enough for comfort and safety.

Program type Sail training for paying trainees. Corporate charters and promotion.

Specs LOA: 96'. LOD: 86'. Draft: 8'. Beam: 16'6". Rig height: 96'. Freeboard: 5'. Sail area: 3,500 sq. ft. Sail no.: 7. Tons: 76 grt. Power: single Volvo 160 hp. Hull: steel. Designer: Bob Johnston. Built: 1984; Kanter Yachts, Port Stanley, Ontario. **Coast Guard cert.** Passenger vessel, Minor Waters II (CCG cert.). **Crew** 6 (including 2 CCG-certified captains). Trainees: 70 (day). Age: all. Sex: co-ed.

Contact Doug Prothero, Captain/Operations Manager, Great Lakes Schooner Co., Suite 111, Toronto, Ontario M5J 2N5 Canada; 800 267-3866; FAX 416 260-6377.

CHANCE

Rig gaff-rigged sloop. **Homeport/waters** Bath, Me.: Kennebec River, Casco Bay.

Program type Sea education in maritime history.

Specs Sparred length: 42'. LOA: 31'. LOD: 31'. LWL: 27'. Draft: 5'. Beam: 10'. Power: Westerbroke diesel. Hull: wood. Built: Wilbur Morse, Friendship, Me.

Contact Ruth Maschino, Director of Public Program, Maine Maritime Museum, 243 Washington St., Bath, ME 04530; 207 443-1316.

Clearwater

Rig gaff topsail sloop. **Homeport/waters** Poughkeepsie, N.Y.: Hudson River, New York Harbor and Long Island Sound.

Who sails? Individuals, families and groups. **Season** April 15 to November 15 (daily education program); winter maintenance program. **Cost** $6-$20 per person/day. $40/week for crew/trainees bunk. $500-$1,500 group rate. Membership is $30/year for individuals, $10 for low income. $30 per week for crew-trainee berth; $600-$1,250 per group for three-hour education sails; $25 per year membership; $7.50 for low income.

The *Clearwater* is the only full-sized replica of the 18th- and 19th-century merchant vessels known as Hudson River sloops. Since 1969, *Clearwater* has served both as a platform for hands-on environmental education and as a symbol for grassroots action. The sloop is owned and operated by Hudson River Sloop Clearwater, Inc., a non-profit membership organization dedicated to defending and restoring the Hudson River and related waterways.

The sloop sails seven days a week, carrying as many as 50 passengers for three- to five-hour education programs. Adults and children take part in a wide range of activities involving water life, water chemistry, sail-raising, steering, piloting and more. A U.S. Coast Guard licensed captain is in charge, and an education specialist directs the program. The permanent crew of first, second and third mates, bosun, engineer, cook and educator are complemented by apprentices aged 16 and older, an education assistant and volunteers. During their month on board, apprentices are given in-depth training in many aspects of sailing and maintaining a wooden ship and in the education program.

Program type Sail training for crew and apprentices. Sea education in marine science, maritime history and ecology. Passenger trade day sails and overnight. Dockside interpretation during port visits. Clientele includes school groups from elementary through college and individuals of all ages.

Specs Sparred length: 106'. LOA: 76'6". LWL: 64'7". Draft: 6'6" (max.); 13'6" (min.). Beam: 24'7". Rig height: 108'. Sail area: 4,305 sq. ft. Tons: 69 grt. Power: diesel. Hull: wood. Designer: Cy Hamlin. Built: 1969; Harvey Gamage Shipyard, South Bristol, Me. **Coast Guard cert**. Passenger vessel (Subchapter T). **Crew** 7. Trainees: 50 (day). Sex: co-ed.

Contact Captain Betsy Garthwaite, Hudson River Sloop Clearwater, Inc., 112 Market St., Poughkeepsie, NY 12601-4095; 914 454-7673; FAX 914 454-7953.

CLIPPER CITY

Rig gaff topsail schooner. **Homeport/waters** Chesapeake Bay (summer); Caribbean Sea (winter).

Who sails? Individuals and groups. **Season** year round.

S/V Clipper City is a replica of a Great Lakes lumber schooner of the same name which sailed from 1854 until 1892. The plans for the *Clipper City* of 1985 were obtained from the Smithsonian Institution and adapted for modern use. *Clipper City* sails Baltimore's Inner Harbor and the waters of the Chesapeake Bay from April through October each year. *Clipper City* provides two- and three-hour public excursions for tourists in the Baltimore area as well as private charters for corporate groups and families. She sails up to 21 times each week and has carried over 25,000 passengers in a single season.

Specs LOA: 158'.
LOD: 120'. Draft: 6' (min.); 14' (max.). Beam: 27'6". Rig height: 135'. Sail area: 10,200 sq. ft. Tons: 210 grt. Power: CAT 3208 SS. Hull: steel. Built: 1985; Jacksonville, Fla.

Contact William L. Blocher, General Manager, Clipper City, Inc., 5022 Campbell Blvd., Suite F, Baltimore, MD 21236; 410 931-6777; FAX 410 931-6705.

COMPASS ROSE

Rig gaff topsail schooner, 2-masted. **Homeport/waters** Ft. Lauderdale, Fla.: New England (summer), Florida coast and Bahamas (winter).

Who sails? Student groups and individuals of all ages. **Season** year round.

Compass Rose's design was based on that of an 18th-century American coastal schooner. For a short time, *Compass Rose* was owned by a well known television personality until the present owner acquired her in 1973. Named for a vessel in Nicholas Monsarrat's celebrated novel *The Cruel Sea*, the *Compass Rose* is used for a variety of different enterprises. With the appearance of a pirate ship, *Compass Rose* has appeared in several movies and documentaries as well as advertising and commercial films. She has also participated in many tall ships festival and historical reenactments. Most important, she has been the platform for a number of environmental research projects. One such project was "Track of the Leatherback," a program to collect information about the largest species of turtle, individual specimens of which weigh up to a ton. Electronic transmitters were installed on the leatherbacks — an endangered species — and surveillance gear on *Compass Rose* tracked their habits and movements through the sea.

Program type Informal in-house programming in environmental studies.

Specs Sparred length: 57'. LOA: 50'. LOD: 47'. LWL: 40'. Draft: 6'. Beam: 14'. Rig height: 55'. Freeboard: 5'. Sail area: 2,200 sq. ft. Tons: 25 grt. Power: 85 hp diesel. Hull: wood. Built: 1969; M. Thygeson, Nova Scotia.

Contact Robert Entin, Olde Ships Inc., PO Box 1339, Newport, RI 02840; 401 849-7988 (summer); Robert Entin, Compass Rose, PO Box 22598, Fort Lauderdale, FL 33335; 305 524-0096 (winter).

CONSTITUTION, USS

Rig ship, three-masted; 44-gun frigate. **Homeport/waters** Charlestown, Mass.: Boston Harbor.

Who sails? Individuals, families and school and other groups. Affiliated institutions include USS Constitution Museum.

"Old Ironsides" is the oldest commissioned warship afloat in the world. One of six ships ordered by President George Washington to protect America's growing maritime interests in the 1790s, *Constitution* earned widespread renown for her ability to punish French privateers in the Caribbean and thwart Barbary pirates of the Mediterranean. The ship's greatest glory came during the War of 1812 when she defeated four British frigates. During her first engagement, against HMS *Guerriére* in 1812, seamen nicknamed her "Old Ironsides" when they saw British cannon balls glance off her 21-thick oak hull.

In the 1830s, the ship was slated to be broken up, but a public outcry sparked by publication of a poem by Oliver Wendell Holmes saved her. Over the following century, the ship undertook many military assignments and served as a barracks and as a training ship. Restored in 1927, after a final coast-to-coast tour, in 1934 *Constitution* was moored in the Charlestown Navy Yard where she is open year round for free public tours.

Program type U.S. naval history.

Specs LOA: 204'. LWL: 172'. Draft: 43'5". Beam: 22'6". Rig height: 220'. Freeboard: 19'. Sail area: originally 42,710 sq. ft. (no longer carries sails). Tons: 2,200 disp. Hull: wood. Built: Oct. 21, 1797; Edmond Hartt Shipyard, Boston, Mass. **Coast Guard cert.** commissioned U.S. Navy ship; National Historical Landmark. Crew 48.

Contact Commander Michael Beck, USN, Executive Officer, USS *Constitution*, Charlestown Navy Yard, Charlestown, MA 02129-1797; 617 242-5670; FAX 617 242-5616.

CORONET

Rig Schooner. **Homeport/waters** Newport, R.I.

The last great American yacht, *Coronet* won the 1887 transatlantic race, and during the first of her four circum-navigations of the world via Cape Horn hosted King Kalakaua of Hawaii and Emperor Meiji Yokohama in 1888. While in Europe her visits included Cowes, Gibraltar, Cherbourg, Toulon, Le Havre and other ports. She was the site of the first Japanese-American scientific expedition to study a total eclipse of the sun.

The 108-year-old yacht *Coronet* has recently been acquired by the International Yacht Restoration School (IYRS) and is about to undergo a complete restoration and refit. The IYRS is a non-profit organization founded in 1993 for the purpose of teaching students the skills, history and related sciences involved in the understanding, restoration and mainte-nance of classic sailing ships. After her restoration, *Coronet* will be ideal for tall ships events as well as serve as a goodwill ambassador for the United States.

Specs Sparred length: 173'. LOA: 133'. LOD: 133'. LWL: 128'. Draft: 11'7". Beam: 27'. Freeboard: 6'. Tons: 174 grt. Hull: wood. Designer: Smith & Terry. Built: 1885; C. & R. Poillon, Brooklyn, N.Y.

Contact Debbie Lennon, International Yacht Restoration School, 28 Church St., Newport, RI 02840; 401 849-3060; FAX 401 849-1492.

DARIABAR

Rig schooner. **Homeport/waters** Sausalito Calif.: California and NE Pacific.

Who sails? College students and adults involved in ocean research.

Dariabar, launched in 1992, is a custom-built sailing research vessel. Her lines are those of a John Alden schooner and her design incorporates both traditional and modern aspects. She is built from steel with watertight subdivisions and a double bottom. She has a generous lab and workspace amidships with lifting gear above deck. *Dariabar* is presently involved in bioacoustic research and marine mammal observation. She is associated with Pelagikos, a California-based marine research organization. Pelagikos, in conjunction with Mendocino College, conducts courses in marine mammal ecology and behavior aboard *Dariabar*. These classes offer students the opportunity to engage in active research while learning about sailing and life at sea. Pelagikos also employs *Dariabar* as a platform for research conducted by other college and scientific organizations.

Program Type Sea education, marine science, ecology and bioacoustic research in cooperation with accredited institutions.

Specs LOA: 84'. LOD: 84'. LWL: 64'. Draft: 10'. Beam: 18'. Rig height: 90'. Freeboard: 6'. Sail area: 3,000 sq. ft. Tons: 85 grt. Power: 6M 6-71 diesel. Hull: steel. Designer: John Alden. Built: E. A. Silva, Oakland, CA. **Coast Guard cert.** Ocean Research Vessel (Subchapter U). **Crew** 4 (educators). Trainees: 30 (day); 10 (overnight). Sex: co-ed.

Contact Urmas Kaldveer, Executive Director, Pelagikos, Sausalito, CA 94966; 707 462-5671; FAX 707 468-3120. E-mail: urmas_kaldveer@redwoodfn.org.

DISCOVERY

Rig Dipping lug. **Homeport/waters** Anacortes, Wash.: Puget Sound, San Juan and Gulf Islands.

Who sails? High school, college groups and individuals aged. **Cost** $90 per person per day.

Coined from the nautical term describing the moment a ship slips its moorings and commits itself to the open sea, Outward Bound is an educational organization dedicated to excellence in adventure-based outdoor education. For 30 years, the school's mission has remained unchanged: to teach respect for self, concern for others, leadership and care for the environment.

The Pacific Crest Outward Bound School operates four longboats: *Discovery, Resolution, Porpoise* and *Elizabeth Bonaventure,* locally crafted replicas of the ship's boats carried by British Captain George Vancouver's *Discovery* on his charting exploration of the Northwest Coast in 1792. Inspected as sailing school vessels, they are extremely seaworthy and safe and each carries a two-masted sailing rig and 10 oars as auxiliary power. Seamanship courses are offered to both youth and adults. Based in Washington State's San Juan Islands, each program is a unique blending of Northwest history, seamanship, and environmental education. As one student wrote: "Our instructors gave us the skill, the San Juans the opportunity and our crew the power to achieve."

Program type Sail training with paying trainees. Sea education in maritime history and ecology. Overnight passages. Dockside interpretation during outport visits.

Specs Sparred length: 25'. LOA: 25'. LOD: 25'. LWL: 23'. Draft: 2'. Beam: 6'. Rig height: 18'. Freeboard: 3'. Sail area: 250 sq. ft. Power: oars. Hull: wood. Designer: Greg Foster. Built: 1987; Greg Foster, Washington. **Coast Guard cert.** Sailing school vessel (Subchapter R). **Crew** 2. Trainees: 10 (overnight). Age: 16+. Sex: co-ed.

Contact Brad Wetmore, Sea Program Director, Pacific Crest Outward Bound School, 508 1/2 Commercial Ave., Anacortes, WA 98221; 360 293-0232.

DOROTHEA

Rig ketch. **Homeport/waters** Halifax, N.S.: coastal Nova Scotia.

Who sails? Individuals and groups associated with accredited schools and colleges — Scouts, the YMCA, Aconcagua Foundation, public and private schools. **Cost** $35 per person per day.

The Nova Scotia Sea School offers a year-round program of traditional wooden boat building joined with sail training in the boats we build. Local students may participate year round, others may come to sail in the summer. Students who return to the school year take on increasing responsibility both in the boat shop and on the water, and pass on what they've learned to others.

We build 28' ketch-rigged open pulling boats based on local design, and take them on coastal expeditions, living in the boat. To be able to build a good boat, well-crafted and seaworthy, and take command of that boat and its crew in open water, students must know something about themselves and others: pride in one's work; care for one's resources; appreciation for one's environment; cooperation; taking responsibility for oneself; overcoming hesitation and working with fear; going beyond personal comfort to benefit others; and compassion.

Without these qualities, the boat will leak and the crew will be clumsy and mutinous. The real world is the real teacher.

Program type Sail training with paying trainees. Sea education programs in marine science, maritime history and ecology, and informal in-house programming.

Specs LOA: 28'6". LOD: 28'6". Draft: 5'. Beam: 7'. Tons: 4. Power: oars/sail. Hull: wood. Designer: E.Y.E. Marine. Built: 1995; Halifax. **Crew** 1 (day); 2 (overnight). Trainees: 10.

Contact Crane W. Stookey, Executive Director, The Nova Scotia Sea School, PO Box 546, Central C.R.O., Halifax, Nova Scotia B35 2S4 Canada; 902 423-7284.

EAGLE, USCG BARQUE

Former name *Horst Wessel.* **Rig** barque, 3-masted. **Homeport/waters** New London, Conn.: Atlantic Ocean, Caribbean and Pacific Ocean.

Who sails? Enrolled cadets at the U.S. Coast Guard Academy. **Season** year round. **Cost** included in school tuition.

One of five sister ships built for sail training in Germany in the 1930s, *Eagle* was included in reparations paid to the United States following World War II, and the Coast Guard took her over as a training ship. Aboard the *Eagle*, cadets have a chance to put into practice the navigation, engineering and other skills they are taught at the Coast Guard Academy ashore. As underclassmen, they fill positions normally taken by the enlisted crew of a ship, including watches at the helm. They handle the more than 20,000 square feet of sail and more than 20 miles of rigging. Over 200 lines must be coordinated during a major ship maneuver, and the cadets must learn the name and function of each line. As upperclassmen, they perform functions normally handled by officers guiding the ship. For many, their tour of duty aboard *Eagle* is their first experience of life at sea; but it is here that they learn to serve as the leaders they will one day become in the Coast Guard.

Program type Seamanship.

Specs Sparred length: 295'. LOA: 266'8". LWL: 231'. Draft: 17'. Beam: 40'. Rig height: 147'4". Sail area: 22,245 sq. ft. (23 sails). Tons: 2,186. Power: 1,000 hp diesel. Hull: steel. Built: 1936; Blohm & Voss, Hamburg, Germany. **Sex:** co-ed.

Contact CAPT Donald F. Grosse, Commanding Officer, U.S. Coast Guard Academy, USCG Barque Eagle (WIX 327), New London, CT 06320; 203 444-8595; FAX 203 444-8445.

EBB TIDE

Rig tops'l schooner. **Homeport/waters** Gloucester, MA.: Gloucester and North Shore waters.

Who sails? Fund development personnel from area non-profit institutions — Salem Maritime National Historic Site, Forbes Museum, etc., and trainees involved in military reenactments and classic sailing events. **Season** April to November.

Ebb Tide is a delightful tops'l schooner, built by Peter Legnos of Legnos Boatbuilding in Groton, CT. Forty feet overall, *Ebb Tide* draws 4'6" with a beam of 10'3". She is quite a sight traveling at 35 mph upwind on her custom boat trailer, making her one of the smallest riggers, making her one of the few trailerable square riggers, and making her one of the few fiberglass boats to carry square sails. Her Volvo engine was replaced last year with a Westerbeke, just enough to get her back to her homeport of Eastern Point Yacht Club. Small, but quick, and undefeated in her division at the marvelous Gloucester Schooner races, she carries quite a bit, with a complement of three ten-gauge and one four-gauge cannons. Her hull is black, her sails are white, and her brightwork is as shiny as her owner has the time to do.

Ebb Tide participates in classic and antique vessel events in the Boston area, as well as reenactment events such as the birthday of the United States Navy in Beverly, MA and the birthday of the United States Coast Guard in Newburyport, MA. *Ebb Tide* is privately owned, and does not offer a "formal" sail training program. but we are always eager for crew in any of our reenactments or classic sailboat events.

Program type Sail training for crew and apprentices. Education in maritime history in the form of military reenactments and gunnery practices   Dockside interpretation.

Specs Sparred length: 40'. LOA: 40'. LOD: 30'. Draft: 4'6". Beam: 10'3". Freeboard: 2'. Tons: 4.5 grt. Power: Westerbeke 6 hp diesel. Hull: fiberglass. Built: 1975; Legnos Boatbuilding, Groton, CT. **Crew** 2. Trainees: 4 (day); 4 (overnight). Age: 16-75. Sex: co-ed. Dockside visitors: 6.

Contact Captain Keating Willcox, *Ebb Tide*, Longmeadow Way, Hamilton, MA 01936-0403; 508 468-3869; FAX 508 468-3869; E-mail: kwillcox@shore.net.

ELISSA

Former names *Pioneer, Achaios, Christophoros, Gustaf, Fjeld, Elissa.* **Rig** bark, 3-masted.
Homeport/waters Galveston, Tex.: Galveston Bay, Gulf of Mexico.

Who sails? School groups from middle school through college, and individuals of all ages.
Season April to November. **Cost** volunteers and guests only.

During her 90-year commercial career, *Elissa*'s riveted iron hull has put to sea under five flags: English, Norwegian, Swedish, Finnish and Greek. Discovered in a Greek scrapper's yard by archaeologist Peter Throckmorton, the ship was purchased by the Galveston Historical Foundation in 1975. Seven years later, *Elissa* put to sea under sail for the first time in decades.

Elissa spends most of her time as a dock-side attraction at the Texas Seaport Museum. Volunteers work to maintain the vessel and interpret her to the tens of thousands of visitors to the museum's dockside demonstrations, overnight youth programs, and special events and festivals. The ship puts to sea every year for a series of day sails in the Gulf of Mexico. Working under professional officers, her all-volunteer crew complete an extensive dockside training program. Each year, 80 to 100 people are put to the test of handling the ship under sail during her trials. She has made longer voyages to other Gulf Coast ports and to New York for Operation Sail 1986/Salute to Liberty.

Program type Sail training for crew and apprentices. Sea education in maritime history based on informal in-house training. Dockside interpretation.

Specs Sparred length: 202'. LOA: 155'. LOD: 150'. Draft: 10'. Beam: 28'. Rig height: 110'. Freeboard: 10'. Sail area: 12,000 sq. ft. Tons: 411 grt. Power: 450 hp diesel. Hull: iron. Built: 1877; Alexander Hall and Sons Yard, Aberdeen, Scotland. **Coast Guard cert.** Passenger vessel (Subchapter T). **Crew** 40. Trainees: 85 (day). Age: 16-75. Sex: co-ed. Dockside visitors: 250.

Contact Kurt Voss, Director, Texas Seaport Museum/Galveston Historical Foundation, 2016 Strand, Galveston, TX 77550; 409 763-1877; FAX 409 765-7851.

ELIZABETH II

Rig bark, three-masted (lateen mizzen). **Homeport/waters** Manteo, N.C.: Inland sounds North Carolina.

Who sails? School groups from elementary school through college, and individuals. **Season** Spring and fall. **Cost** $3.00 for adults, $2.00 senior citizens, $1.50 students (dockside visits).

Built with private funds to commemorate America's 400th anniversary, *Elizabeth II* is named for a vessel that sailed from Plymouth, England, on the second of the three Roanoke voyages sponsored by Sir Walter Raleigh between 1584 and 1587. She probably carried marines, colonists and supplies to be used in establishing a military garrison to support England's claim to the New World.

Elizabeth II's sail training program is designed to give volunteer crew the opportunity to learn about and preserve our 16th-century maritime heritage. In addition to classroom instruction and dockside training, crew members also participate in the care and maintenance of wooden vessels. The 24-foot ship's boat, *Silver Chalice*, is used for underway training and travels with *Elizabeth II* when she sails. Voyages are scheduled during the spring and fall seasons. Sponsorship for the volunteer crew program is provided by the Friends of Elizabeth II, Inc., a non-profit organization dedicated to supporting the admission, guest passes, ship's store discounts and the newsletter, "Bosn's Call."

Program type Sail training for crew and apprentices. Dockside interpretation.

Specs Sparred length: 78'. LOA: 68'6". LOD: 55'. LWL: 59'. Draft: 8'. Beam: 16'6". Rig height: 65'. Sail area: 1,920 sq. ft. Tons: 97 grt. Hull: wood. Designer: W. A. Baker and Stanley Potter. Built: 1983; O. Lie-Nielsen, Creef-Davis Shipyard, Manteo, N.C. Age: 16+. Sex: co-ed and single-sex.

Contact William H. Rea, Executive Director, Elizabeth II State Historic Site, PO Box 155, Manteo, NC 27954; 919 473-1144; FAX 919 473-1483.

ENDEAVOUR

Rig J-Class yacht. **Homeport/waters** Newport, R.I.

Season year round. **Cost** $15,000 per day.

Built for Sir T. O. M. Sopwith's first challenge for the America's Cup in 1934, *Endeavour* failed to capture the cup, though she came closer than any other vessel to that time, and she was renowned as the most beautiful of the J-boats. Over the next 46 years, *Endeavour* came close to the scrapyard several times, but in 1984 she was acquired by Elizabeth Meyer who undertook a five-year restoration of the yacht. With a richly appointed interior reminiscent of yachting's heyday at the turn of the century, *Endeavour* is the largest sloop-rigged vessel sailing today, spreading 9,000 square feet of canvas under full sail. Powerful, finely balanced and fast, sailing *Endeavour* has been compared with "riding a 747 bareback." Since the completion of her refit, *Endeavour* has sailed more than 50,000 miles and carried more than 2,000 passengers in North America, Europe and the Mediterranean. There are plans to increase the scope of her voyaging, and perhaps even undertake a circumnavigation.

Specs Sparred length: 228'. LOA: 130'. Draft: 15'8". Beam: 22'. Rig height: 165'. Sail area: 7,500 sq. ft. Tons: 160 grt. Power: 400 hp 3406 Caterpillar diesel. Hull: steel. Designer: Charles Nicholson. Built: 1934; Camper & Nicholsons, England. **Crew** 8.

Contact Elizabeth E. Meyer, J Class Management, 28 Church St., Newport, RI 02840; 401 849-3060; FAX 401 849-1642.

ERNESTINA

Former name *Effie M. Morrissey.* **Rig** gaff topsail schooner, 2-masted. **Homeport/waters** New Bedford, Mass.: East Coast, Canada (summer); Caribbean and West Africa.

Who sails? School groups from elementary through college, and individuals of all ages. Affiliated institutions include public schools in New Bedford, Martha's Vineyard, Boston and Gloucester and P.A.L.M.S. Activity — Massachusetts Department of Education. **Season** year round. **Cost** $125 per person per day; $3,000 group rate or charter per day.

Originally named *Effie M. Morrissey*, the *Fredonia*-style fishing schooner *Ernestina* fished the Grand Banks for 34 years. In 1925, Captain Bob Bartlett bought her for Arctic exploration and she went north for the next 20 years, including a stint in the U.S. Navy during World War II. Purchased by Captain Henrique Mendes, she was the last regular Atlantic sailing packet and made 12 8,000-mile round trips from the Cape Verde Islands to southern New England carrying goods and passengers until 1965. In 1982, the Republic of Cape Verde gave her to the Commonwealth of Massachusetts to symbolize the close ties between the lands, with the stipulation that she be used for seafaring education. Today, the fully restored *Ernestina* is inspected and certified by the U.S. Coast Guard as an ocean-going sailing school vessel and carries 25 trainees and nine professional crew. Her training and sea experience programs include organizational leadership seminars, public and private school trips, recreational sail training for adults, high-impact drug awareness and therapy programs and special interest offshore voyages.

Program type Sea education in marine science, maritime history and ecology in cooperation with accredited schools and colleges, Scouts and other groups. Passengers carried on day and overnight sails. Dockside interpretation.

Specs Sparred length: 156'. LOA: 112'. LWL: 94'. Draft: 13'. Beam: 24'5". Rig height: 115'. Sail area: 8,323 sq. ft. Tons: 120. Power: 259 hp diesel. Hull: wood. Designer: George M. McClain. Built: 1894; Tarr and James Shipyard, Essex, Mass. **Coast Guard cert.** Sailing school vessel (Subchapter R); passenger vessel (Subchapter T). **Crew** 11. Trainees: 80 (day); 24 (overnight). Dockside visitors: 100.

Contact Gregg Swanzey, Executive Director, Schooner Ernestina Commission, PO Box 2010, New Bedford, MA 02741-2010; 508 992-4900; FAX 508 984-7719.

Fair Jeanne

Rig Brigantine. **Homeport/waters** Kingston, Ont.: Great Lakes, Maritime Provinces, Caribbean. **Cost** Inquire.

Who sails? Students and others aged 13 to 24.

Built in 1982, the *Fair Jeanne* is a 100-foot brigantine originally built by the late Captain Thomas G. Fuller as a private yacht. Carrying 4,000 square feet of sail, the ship is now in service as a sail training vessel serving youths aged 13 to 24 under the Bytown Brigantine flag. Operating out of Kingston, Ontario, during the summer months, the ship will voyage the Great Lakes, St. Lawrence Seaway, and, during the winter months, will carry students on voyages in the Caribbean tracing historical maritime and naval events. Carrying a ship's company of 21 trainees plus crew, the sail training program reflects Captain Fuller's belief in using sail training as a means of building confidence and resourcefulness in our youth. Thomas Fuller was one of Canada's most decorated war heroes, earning the name "Pirate of the Adriatic" and holding the distinction of the longest time served in offensive war action. Thomas Fuller founded the non-profit Bytown Brigantine, Inc., in 1984 to provide traditional sail training to local youths.

Program type Sail training with paying trainees. Sea education in maritime history in cooperation with organized groups. Dockside interpretation.

Specs Sparred length: 120'. LOA: 110'. LOD: 82'. LWL: 62'. Draft: 6' (min.); 13' (max.). Beam: 24'6". Rig height: 80'. Freeboard: 8'. Sail area: 4,000 sq. ft. Tons: 135 grt. Power: GM 671. Hull: steel & fiberglass. Designer: T. G. Fuller. Built: 1982; T. G. Fuller, Ottawa, Ont. **Crew** 10; 1 instructor. Trainees: 21 (overnight).

Contact Captain Alexander G. Mulder, Executive Director, Bytown Brigantine, Inc., 2700 Queenstown Dr., Ottawa, Ontario K2B 8H6 Canada; 613 820-6000; FAX 613 596-5947.

FEDERALIST

Rig bark, 3-masted. **Homeport/waters** Alexandria, Va.: inland bays and rivers; and on-land exhibits.

Who sails? Students and others, Pre-school and older. **Season** year round.

Federalist is a full-size replica of a miniature ship built in Baltimore in 1788 to celebrate the state of Maryland's ratification of the United States Constitution. Under the command of Captain Joshua Barney, the original *Federalist* sailed from Baltimore to Mount Vernon where she was presented to General George Washington as a gift from the merchants of Baltimore. She sank in a hurricane a short time later.

The replica *Federalist* was built by members of the Potomac Maritime Historical Society, formed in 1987 to promote public awareness of our maritime heritage. Since then, she has participated in many nautical events in Alexandria and elsewhere. Despite her small size, the replica *Federalist* is a fully operational square-rigged sailing vessel, equipped with a 3.5 hp engine. Unlike her larger sisters, however, *Federalist* is also at home on land. She frequently participates in street parades, riding on a decorated trailer and pulled by her crew using special traces. For period events such as the George Washington birthday parade, the crew marches in 18th-century sailors' uniforms.

Program type Maritime history.

Specs Sparred length: 25'. LOA: 17'. LOD: 15'. LWL: 13'. Draft: 2'. Beam: 5'. Rig height: 19'. Freeboard: 1'6". Sail area: 90 sq. ft. Tons: 500 lb. displacement. Power: 3.5 hp engine. Hull: wood. Built: 1987; The Potomac Maritime Historical Society, Inc. **Coast Guard cert.** None required. **Crew** 4-6. Trainees: 2-3. Age: 4+ (on-land instruction); 12+ (on-water instruction). Sex: co-ed.

Contact Stanley Martin, President, Alexandria Seaport Foundation, 1000 South Lee Street, Jones Point, Alexandria, VA 22320; 703 549-7078; FAX 703 549-6715; E-mail: ASFHQS@aol.com.

FRANCIS TODD

Rig gaff topsail schooner, 2-masted. **Homeport/waters** Bar Harbor, Me.: coastal Maine.

Who sails? School groups from elementary school through college as well as individuals and families.

The *Francis Todd* was originally built as a sardine carrier for the Stinson Canning Company, and she spent over 40 years in the herring fishery. Although built as a power vessel, her hull model was similar to that of the earlier auxiliary schooners in the sardine trade. Later rigged for both seining and carrying, this vessel navigated the Maine coast in all weathers. Retired from fishery work in 1991, the vessel was purchased by Captain Pagels and underwent a two-year rebuilding. Re-rigged as a two-masted topsail schooner, the *Francis Todd* is admired as a handy and handsome vessel. The *Francis Todd* is based in Bar Harbor and sails the Maine coast and the shores of Acadia National Park on day sails.

Program type Sail training for crew and apprentices. Passenger day sails. Dockside interpretation.

Specs Sparred length: 101'. LOD: 78'. Draft: 7'6". Beam: 17'6". Rig height: 80'. Sail area: 2,800 sq. ft. Tons: 53 grt. Power: diesel. Hull: wood. Designer: Newbert & Wallace. Built: 1947; Newbert & Wallace, Thomaston, Maine. **Coast Guard cert.** Passenger vessel (Subchapter T). **Crew** 3. Trainees: 81. Age: all. Sex: co-ed.

Contact Captain Steven F. Pagels, Downeast Windjammer Cruises, PO Box 8, Cherryfield, ME 04622; 207 546-2927; FAX 207 546-2023.

FYRDRACA

Rig Viking longship. **Homeport/waters** Oakley, Md.: Potomac River and Chesapeake Bay.

Who sails? School groups from elementary school through college as well as individuals of all ages. **Season** March to November.

Fyrdraca is a 30'-long, single-masted vessel based on the design of a small ninth-century warship excavated on the German island of Rugen in the Baltic Sea. *Fyrdraca* and the faering boat *Gyrfalcon*, modeled on a vessel found with the ninth-century Norwegian Gokstad ship, frequently work in consort at marine parades and festivals, and they are also used in conjunction with public demonstrations with the Markland Medieval Mercenary Militia's Viking Camp. The Longship Company, Ltd., is a member-supported, non-profit educational institution.

Program type Sail training for crew and apprentices. Sea education in maritime history based on informal in-house programming. Non-paying passengers for day sails. Dockside interpretation.

Specs Sparred length: 34'. LOA: 32'. LWL: 29'. Draft: 2'. Beam: 9'2". Rig height: 25'. Freeboard: 2'6". Sail area: 240 sq. ft. Tons: 6 grt. Hull: wood. Designer: traditional Norse. Built: 1979; Hans Pederson & Sons, Keyport, N.J. **Crew** 6-12 (day); 12-18 (overnight). Trainees: 4-12. Age: 14+. Sex: co-ed. Dockside visitors: 24.

Contact Fred Blounder, President, Longship Company, Ltd., Box 81, Oakley Road, Avenue, MD 20609; 301 390-4089; E-mail: fred@nasirc.hq.nasa.gov.

GAZELA OF PHILADELPHIA

Former name *Gazela Primeiro*. **Rig** barkentine, 3-masted. **Homeport/waters** Penn's Landing, Philadelphia, Pa.: Delaware River and Atlantic Coast.

Who sails? Volunteers who support the maintenance of the ship. Dockside visitors include school groups from elementary school through college, as well as individuals and families.

The *Gazela of Philadelphia* is the oldest wooden square-rigged sailing vessel still in operation. *Gazela of Philadelphia* was built as a Grand Banks fishing vessel, one of a large number of Portuguese ships that fished for cod in that area for hundreds of years. She is currently owned and operated by the Philadelphia Ship Preservation Guild, a private, non-profit organization and sails as a goodwill ambassador for the City of Philadelphia, the Commonwealth of Pennsylvania and the Ports of Philadelphia and Camden (N.J.) at significant events worldwide. *Gazela of Philadelphia* is open to the public on weekends when at Penn's Landing, from May 15 to September 15.

She is maintained and sailed by a very active and knowledgeable volunteer group who participate in sail training activities throughout the year. After 25 hours of work on the vessel, they are eligible for a crew position on the next available cruise. An educational grant permits the teaching of young people 16 years and older many of whom go on to become volunteer crew.

Program type Sail training for crew and apprentices. Sea education based on informal, in-house programming. Dockside interpretation during outport visits.

Specs Sparred length: 178'. LOA: 150'. LOD: 140'. LWL: 133'. Draft: 16'. Beam: 27'9". Rig height: 100'. Sail area: 8,910 sq. ft. Tons: 299 grt. Power: diesel. Hull: wood. Built: 1883; master shipwrights in Cacilhas, Portugal. **Coast Guard cert.** Attraction vessel and uninspected yacht. **Crew** 35 (volunteer). Age: 18-72. Sex: co-ed. Dockside visitors: 135.

Contact Karen H. Love, Executive Vice President, Philadelphia Ship Preservation Guild, Penn's Landing, Columbus Blvd. at Chestnut St., Philadelphia, PA 19106; 215 923-9030; FAX 215 923-2801.

GERONIMO

Rig yawl. **Homeport/waters** Newport, R.I.: North Atlantic and Caribbean.

Who sails? Enrolled 10th-12th grade students at St. George's School. **Season** year round. **Cost** regular school tuition (winter); inquire for summer cruises.

Geronimo makes three six-to-eight day trips during the school year, carrying students from St. George's School. Marine biology and English are taught on board, and the students continue their other courses by correspondence with the faculty at St. George's. Students receive full academic credit for their time on board. The winter cruises usually include operations along the eastern seaboard and in the waters of the Bahamas and northern Caribbean.

Geronimo's primary marine biology research has always included tagging sharks and collecting biological samples for the Apex Predator Investigation of the National Marine Fisheries Service. *Geronimo* also tags sea turtles in cooperation with the Center for Sea Turtle Research of the University of Florida.

In the summer, *Geronimo* makes two four-week cruises, usually to the waters south of New England and around Bermuda. Each summer cruise includes a series of lectures on marine biology and fisheries management. In 1987, *Geronimo* made a transatlantic research cruise to study sea turtles and sharks in the eastern Atlantic and undertake tagging projects in the Azores, Spain and Portugal.

Program type Full curriculum academics, marine biology, environmental studies for high school students.

Specs Sparred length: 61'. LOA: 54'. LWL: 36'. Draft: 8'11". Beam: 13'. Rig height: 63'6". Sail area: 1,433 sq. ft. Tons: 22 grt. Power: diesel. Hull: aluminum. Designer: William Tripp. Built: 1965; Abeking & Rasmussen, West Germany. **Coast Guard cert.** Sailing school vessel (Subchapter R). **Crew** 2-3. Trainees: 6-7. Sex: co-ed.

Contact Captain Stephen Connell, St. George's School, Purgatory Road, PO Box 1910, Newport, RI 02840; 401 847-7565; FAX 401 848-0420.

Gleam

Rig 12-meter sloop. **Homeport/waters** Newport, R.I.: Narragansett Bay.

Who sails? Corporations who charter the vessel for team building and client entertaining.

The eleventh 12-meter vessel built in the United States, *Gleam* is beautifully restored and has her original pre-World War II interior. Together with her near sister ship *Northern Light*, *Gleam* offers a unique team-building program called "Your own America's Cup Regatta." Each boat accommodates 13 guests plus 3 crew members. No previous sailing experience is necessary to participate. Group and corporate outings are available in Newport, Rhode Island, and other New England ports.

Program type Sail training with paying trainees. Passenger day sails.

Specs Sparred length: 67'11". LOA: 67'11". LOD: 67'11". LWL: 46'11". Draft: 9'. Beam: 12'. Rig height: 90'. Freeboard: 3'. Sail area: 1,900 sq. ft. Tons: 30 grt. Power: aux. diesel. Hull: wood. Designer: Clinton Crane and Olin Stephens. Built: 1937; Henry Nevins, City Island, N.Y. **Coast Guard cert**. Passenger vessel (Subchapter T). **Crew** 3. Trainees: 14.

Contact Elizabeth Tiedemann, Director of Sales & Marketing, Seascope Systems, Inc., PO Box 119, 27 Rhode Island Ave., Newport, RI 02840; 401 847-5007, 401 849-6140.

GLENN L. SWETMAN

Rig gaff topsail schooner, 2-masted. **Homeport/waters** Biloxi, Miss.: coastwise Gulf of Mexico.

Who sails? Affiliated institutions include William Carey College. **Season** year round. **Cost** $15 per adult or $10 per child (2-1/2 hours). $750 per day, group rate; $500 for 1/2 day.

The *Glenn L. Swetman* is the first of two replica Biloxi oyster schooners built by the Biloxi Schooner Project under the auspices of the Maritime and Seafood Industry Museum. The *Glenn L. Swetman* is available for charter trips in the Mississippi Sound and to the barrier islands, Cat Island, Horn Island and Ship Island. Walk-up "day sailing" trips are made when she is not under charter. Groups of up to 49 passengers can learn about the maritime and seafood heritage of the Gulf Coast and about the vessels that got Biloxi's seafood industry started. The *Glenn L. Swetman* is an integral part of the museum's Sea and Sail Summer Camp, and sailing classes are also offered through local colleges. In addition, *Glenn L. Swetman* accommodates weddings, parties, and Elderhostel and school groups.

Money for construction and equipping the *Glenn L. Swetman* and her sister ship, *Mike Sekul*, has come from donations by interested individuals, businesses, civic groups and a variety of museum-sponsored fund-raising events.

Program type Maritime history for college students and adults, children's summer camp, and private charters.

Specs Sparred length: 76'. LOA: 65'. LOD: 50'. LWL: 47'. Draft: 4'6". Beam: 17'. Freeboard: 4'6". Sail area: 2,400 sq. ft. Tons: 21 grt. Power: 4-71 Detroit diesel. Built: 1989; William T. Holland, Biloxi, Miss. **Coast Guard cert.** Passenger vessel (Subchapter T). **Crew** 3. Trainees: 49 (day). Age: 15+. Sex: co-ed. Dockside visitors: 49.

Contact Robin Krohn, Manager, Maritime and Seafood Industry Museum, Inc., PO Box 1907, Biloxi, MS 39533; 601 435-6320; FAX 601 435-6309.

GOVERNOR STONE

Rig gaff schooner, 2-masted. **Homeport/waters** Apalachicola, Fla.: Gulf of Mexico, upper coast.

Who sails? School groups from elementary school through college as well as individuals and families. Affiliated institutions include Gulf Coast Community College, Panama City, Fla. **Season** year round. **Cost** $20 per person per day; $900 group rate; $450 half day. Overnight trips by special arrangements.

The *Governor Stone* was built for Charles Greiner in Pascagoula, Mississippi, in 1877 for use as a cargo freighter, and named for John Marshall Stone, the first elected Governor of Mississippi after the Civil War. This gaff-rigged, shallow draft schooner represents a class of sailing vessels unique to the Gulf Coast. Possibly the last of her type, the *Governor Stone* has seen varied service from an oyster-buy boat to yacht club committee boat to pleasure craft. The *Governor Stone* has been declared a National Historic Landmark by the National Park Service. As the oldest vessel of the American south afloat, and as a representative of a class of vessels unique to the Gulf Coast, she richly deserves this recognition.

Sailing times vary, however we do sail year -round. Reservations are suggested. Reservations and sailing time can be obtained by calling the Apalachicola Maritime Museum.

Program type Sea education in marine science, maritime history and ecology based on informal in-house programming, with special attention given to at-risk students. Passenger day sails and overnight passages. Dockside interpretation.

Specs Sparred length: 68'. LOA: 44'. LOD: 42'. LWL: 38'. Draft: 2'6". Beam: 13'6". Rig height: 52' (35' with lowered topmast). Freeboard: 5'. Sail area: 1,400 sq. ft. Tons: 12 grt. Power: 80 hp diesel. Hull: wood. Built: 1877; Pascagoula, Miss. **Coast Guard cert.** Passenger vessel (Subchapter T) and documented commercial vessel in coastwise fishery. **Crew** 3; 1 instructor. Trainees: 6. Age: 10+. Sex: co-ed.

Contact Connie Stefanko, Assistant Administrator, Apalachicola Maritime Museum, Inc., PO Box 625, Apalachicola, FL 32329-0625; 904 653-8708.

Gyrfalcon

Rig Viking faering boat. **Homeport/waters** Oakley, Md.: Potomac River and Chesapeake Bay. **Season** March to November. **Cost** $20 annual dues.

Who sails? School groups from elementary school through college as well as individuals of all ages. **Season** March to November.

The *Gyrfalcon*, a replica of the smallest of the 9th century Gokstad Ship's faering boats, was built by the Hampton Mariners Museum in Beaufort North Carolina under the direction of Geoffrey Scofield. The *Gyrfalcon* and her sister ship, the *Fyrdraca*, are both owned and operated by The Longship Company, Ltd., a member-supported, non-profit educational institution. Both vessels frequently work in concert

at maritime parades, waterfront concerts, and festivals. They also provide public demonstrations with the Markland Medieval Mercenary Militia's Viking Camp, where the public can be treated to crews dressed in historic costume and armor while engaging in historical interpretation.

As an enticement to school children and adults to discover more about the early medieval period, offseason *Gyrfalcon* is frequently found as a display in area schools and libraries.

Program type Sail training for crew and apprentices. Dockside interpretation at outport visits.

Specs LOA: 20'. Draft: 1'. Beam: 5'. Rig height: 12'. Freeboard: 1'. Sail area: 80 sq. ft. Tons: 200 lb. Power: four 9' oars. Hull: wood. Designer: traditional. Built: 1981; Beaufort Mariners Museum, Beaufort, N.C. **Coast Guard cert.** Uninspected yacht. **Crew** 3-5. Trainees: 1-3. Age: 14+. Sex: co-ed.

Contact Fred Blonder, The Longship Company, Ltd., Box 81 Oakley Road, Avenue, MD 20609; 301 390-4089; E-mail: fred@nasirc.hq.nasa.gov.

HALVE MAEN

Rig ship, 3-masted. **Homeport/waters** Croton-on-Hudson, N.Y.: East Coast and Great Lakes.

Who sails? School groups from elementary school through high school, individuals and adults.

The replica ship *Halve Maen* (Half Moon) was launched on June 20, 1989, to draw attention to the Dutch role in exploring and colonizing America. Since then, she has visited over 40 ports along the eastern seaboard and the Great Lakes and has been visited by well over 200,000 visitors. The ship is based on careful historical research of original Dutch East India Company documents, including the resolution of 1608 ordering the original ship's construction. Under the command of Henry Hudson, that ship sailed up the Hudson River to as far as present-day Albany in 1609, a voyage that lead to the founding of the colony of Nieu Nederland in 1614.

The *Halve Maen* takes visitors back to the Age of Exploration, and her crew strive to expand people's knowledge of maritime history and the sea. Our program is unique in that while we have an active sail training program, our chief object is presenting history to the public. We therefore require crew to become competent in historical presentation as well as in shiphandling.

Program type Sail training and maritime history based on informal in-house programming. Dockside interpretation.

Specs Sparred length: 95'. LOA: 65'. LOD: 64'3". LWL: 84'. Draft: 8'5". Beam: 17'6". Rig height: 78'. Freeboard: 10'5". Sail area: 2,757. Tons: 112 grt. Power: aux. diesel. Hull: wood. Designer: Nick Benton. Built: 1989; Nick Benton, Albany, N.Y. **Coast Guard cert.** Attraction vessel. **Crew** 7-12 (day); 8-15 (overnight). Dockside visitors: 48.

Contact Nick Burlakoff, Museum Director, New Netherland Museum, 181 South Riverside Ave., Croton-on-Hudson, NY 10520; 914 923-1351.

HAROLD K. ACKER

Rig cutter. **Homeport/waters** Cobb Island, Md.: Lower Potomac River, Chesapeake Bay.

Who sails? Students and adults. **Season** April to October **Cost** $70 per person per day.

The *Harold K. Acker* operates as a day and weekend charter vessel in the lower Potomac River and Chesapeake Bay. Her program specializes in small-group youth training with emphasis on teamwork, responsibility and respecting the needs of others. Groups are responsible for the daily operation and maintenance of the vessel under the supervision of her master and mate. This includes sailing and piloting as well as meal planning and preparation. One- and two-week winter season charters can also be arranged. The *Harold K. Acker* is a participant in most of the Potomac River and Chesapeake Bay area waterfront festivals. Captain Gardner is a past member of the ASTA board of directors and is fully committed to the ASTA philosophy.

Program type Sail training for crew and apprentices. Passenger day sails and overnight passages.

Specs Sparred length: 39'6". LOA: 34'. LOD: 34'6". LWL: 29'6". Draft: 5'2". Beam: 10'3". Rig height: 47'6". Freeboard: 3'. Sail area: 741 sq. ft. Tons: 8 grt. Power: 34 hp diesel. Hull: fiberglass. Designer: J. W. Gardner/Ta Chiao. Built: 1978; Ta Chiao Shipyards, Taiwan. **Coast Guard cert.** Uninspected yacht. **Crew** 1-2. Trainees: 4 (day); 2 (overnight). Age: all. Sex: co-ed. Dockside visitors: 6.

Contact Captain John Wesley Gardner, SV *Harold K. Acker*, 3105 Weller Rd., Silver Spring, MD 20906; 301 946-0621.

HARVEY GAMAGE

Rig gaff topsail schooner, 2-masted. **Homeport/waters** Boston, Mass.: New England to the Caribbean.

Who sails? School groups from middle school through college, as well as individuals and families. **Season** year round. **Cost** varies with program.

The schooner *Harvey Gamage* offers an array of sea education programs ranging from high school semesters-at-sea to special programs performed in partnership with schools and youth groups. All programs use the power of the sea and the challenge of traditional seafaring as the basis for the shipboard educational curriculum. Ocean Classroom, our high school semester-at-sea, is a true voyage of discovery for qualified sophomores, juniors and seniors. Young people from all over the United States join the ship for this outstanding learning adventure. On a voyage that covers more than 4,000 nautical miles, connecting the Caribbean Sea to the shores of New England, these students live and work as sailors while studying maritime history, literature, science, applied mathematics, writing and navigation.

In the summer, the *Harvey Gamage* sails the waters of New England, offering our Seafaring Camp program to teens ages 13 to 17. Seafaring Camp combines a schooner adventure with an introduction to field work marine biology.

Program type Sail training with paying trainees. Fully accredited sea education in marine science, maritime history, and ecology. Passengers carried for day sails. Dockside interpretation.

Specs Sparred length: 131'. LOA: 95'. LOD: 90'. LWL: 85'. Draft: 9'7". Beam: 23'7". Rig height: 91'. Sail area: 4,200 sq. ft. Tons: 94 grt. Power: 220 hp diesel. Hull: wood. Designer: McCurdy & Rhodes. Built: 1973; Harvey Gamage Shipyard, South Bristol, Maine. **Coast Guard cert.** Passenger vessel (Subchapter T). **Crew** 8. Instructors: 1-3. Trainees: 69 (day); 27 (overnight). Age: all. Sex: co-ed. Dockside visitors: 75.

Contact Bert Rogers, Director, Schooner Harvey Gamage Foundation, Inc., PO Box 60, Francestown, NH 03043; 603 547-2702, 800 724-7245; FAX 603 547-8802.

HAWAIIAN CHIEFTAIN

Rig square topsail ketch. **Homeport/waters** Sausalito, Calif.: San Francisco Bay (summer); southern California coast (winter).

Who sails? School groups from elementary through college as well as individual and families of all ages. Affiliated institutions include National Maritime Museum Association. Orange County Marine Institution. **Season** year round. **Cost** $25 to $100 per person per day; $700-$2,000 group rate.

The *Hawaiian Chieftain* is a 103-foot square topsail ketch built in Hawaii and based in Sausalito, California. A replica of a northern European coastal trading vessel from the 1790s, she is a fine example of a contemporary interpretation of traditional design, and is an excellent classroom for the teaching of traditional sailing skills and techniques. Through a variety of on-the-water day programs, the professional crew works closely with the cadets and passengers to provide a hands-on educational sailing experience. The *Hawaiian Chieftain* coordinates with other organizations such as the San Francisco Maritime Museum Association and the Sea Training Institute to extend the opportunity for Bay Area school children to participate in unique experiences that both promote the learning of skills normally unavailable to them, and develop their self-esteem in a challenging environment. One integral part of this is an experiential program of awareness and conservation of San Francisco Bay's delicate ecosystem. The *Hawaiian Chieftain* also offers sail training for adults, private charters, and natural history cruises. Her distinctive presence has become a familiar sight on the windy waters of the Bay.

Program type Sail training with paying trainees. Sea education in marine science, maritime history and ecology in cooperation with accredited schools and colleges. Passenger day sails. Dockside interpretation.

Specs Sparred length: 103'. LOA: 78'. LOD: 65'. LWL: 62'. Draft: 6'. Beam: 22'. Rig height: 75'. Freeboard: 3'. Sail area: 4,200 sq. ft. Tons: 64 grt. Power: twin Volvo diesels. Hull: steel. Designer: Raymond R. Richards. Built: 1988; Lahaina Welding Co., Lahaina, Maui, Hawaii. **Coast Guard cert.** Passenger vessel (Subchapter T). **Crew** 6 (day); 10 (overnight). Trainees: 49. Age: all. Sex: co-ed. Dockside visitors: 60.

Contact Captain Ian McIntyre, Hawaiian Chieftain Inc., Suite #266, 3020 Bridgeway, Sausalito, CA 94965; 415 331-3214; FAX 415 331-9415.

Heritage of Miami II

Rig square topsail schooner, 2-masted. **Homeport/waters** Miami, Fla.: Biscayne Bay, Florida Keys, Gulf of Mexico.

Who sails? School groups from elementary school through college as well as individuals. Affiliated institutions include Dade County Schools, Broward County Schools, area private schools and the Boy Scouts of America. **Season** year round. **Cost** $75 per person per day; $1,000 group rate.

The *Heritage of Miami II* is an 83' square topsail schooner that is modern in its materials and construction but traditional in its style. Built specifically for crossing wide expanses of open water, she has a wide, spacious deck that provides ample room for working the sails, lounging in the sun and sleeping in the evening. Her shoal draft makes even small islands accessible while her long bowsprit, topmasts and yards allow extra sails for speed between them.

Heritage of Miami II's travels take her to Garden Key and the famous Fort Jefferson in the Dry Tortugas, the coral reefs of the Florida Keys, and Key West. Sea Explorer cruises last for six days and five nights. Her professional captain and crew help the Explorers experience the life of the sea: setting and furling sails, manning the helm, even catching, cleaning and cooking fish. The program offers a unique opportunity to explore a part of the Florida Keys while enjoying the hands-on nature of this sailing experience.

Program type Sail training for crew, apprentices and paying trainees. Sea education in maritime history and ecology in cooperation with accredited schools and colleges and other organized groups. Passenger day sails and overnight passages. Dockside interpretation.

Specs Sparred length: 85'. LOA: 68'. LOD: 65'. LWL: 62'. Draft: 6'. Beam: 17'9". Rig height: 64'. Freeboard: 8'. Sail area: 2,200 sq. ft. Tons: 47 grt. Power: Ford Lehman 140 hp diesel. Hull: steel. Designer: Merritt Walters. Built: 1988; Howdy Bailey, Norfolk, Va.

Contact Captain Joseph A. Maggio, The Schooner Heritage of Miami, Inc., 3145 Virginia St., Coconut Grove, FL 33133; 305 442-9697; FAX 305 442-9697.

INLAND SEAS

Rig gaff schooner, 2-masted. **Homeport/waters** Suttons Bay, Mich.: Grand Traverse Bay, Lake Michigan.

Who sails? Affiliated institutions include the Great Lakes Maritime Academy and Eastern Michigan University. **Season** spring and summer.

The Inland Seas Association's schooner *Inland Seas* was launched in 1994 to be a hands-on laboratory for students to learn about the Great Lakes. The schooner is steel hulled with detailing similar to traditional tall ships. The vessel is equipped with scientific gear for studying the Great Lakes ecosystem. ISEA's popular Schoolship Program, which began in 1989, offers half-day Great Lakes education opportunities for students aboard *Inland Seas* and chartered schooners *Malabar* and *Manitou*. A variety of summer shipboard programs are offered for students and adults aboard *Inland Sea*, all of which foster an appreciation for and a commitment to the natural and cultural heritage of the Great Lakes.

Program type Marine science and ecology for students from elementary school through college, adults and youth-at-risk.

Specs Sparred length: 80'. LOD: 61'6". LWL: 53'. Draft: 6'6". Beam: 17'. Rig height: 66'. Freeboard: 3'6". Sail area: 1,800 sq. ft. Tons: 41 grt. Power: 130 hp. Hull: steel. Designer: Charles W. Wittholz, Woodin & Marean. Built: 1994; Treworgy Yachts, Palm Coast, FL. **Coast Guard cert.** Passenger vessel (Subchapter T). **Crew** 5. Trainees: 30 (day); 11 (overnight). Age: 11+. Sex: co-ed.

Contact Thomas M. Kelly, Executive Director, Inland Seas Education Association, PO Box 218, Suttons Bay, MI 49682; 616 271-3077; FAX 616 271-3088. E-mail: ISEA@traverse.com.

ISABELLE

Rig ketch. **Homeport/waters** Newport, RI: Southern New England.

Who sails? Adults and families. **Cost** $1,400 per day at group rate.

Isabelle is a classic yacht built and designed in 1924 by the renowned William Fife. Her construction is teak over sawn-oak frames. *Isabelle* is a beautiful reminder of the glamour and romance of the "Golden Age" of yachting.

Since 1978 *Isabelle* has been owned and operated as a day and term charter vessel out of Newport, RI. Her crew includes a master and two deckhands who are fully involved in the maintenance and upkeep of this classic vessel. *Isabelle* is available for port and maritime festivals throughout Southern New England.

Program Type Sail training for crew/apprentices, marine sciences and informal in-house programming. Passenger day sails and dockside interpretation during port visits.

Specs Sparred length: 83'. LOA: 83'. LOD: 83'. LWL: 65'. Draft: 10'5". Beam: 18'. Freeboard: 4'. Sail area: 3,000 sq. ft. Tons: 96 grt. Power: aux. sail. Hull: wood. Designer: William Fife & Sons. Built: 1924; William Fife, Scotland. **Coast Guard cert.** pending. **Crew** 3 (days); 6 (overnight). Trainees: 25 (days); 8 (overnight).

Contact Captain Steve Vaitses, Katama Yachts, Inc., 119 Grove Street, Clinton, CT 06413; 203 669-5921; FAX 203 669-6143.

JOHN E. PFRIEM

Former name *J. N. Carter.* **Rig** Chesapeake Bay bugeye ketch. **Homeport/waters** Bridgeport, Conn.: Long Island Sound.

Who sails? Affiliated institutions include the University of Bridgeport, Housatonic Community College, and seven Connecticut school districts. **Season** April to November.

The *John E. Pfriem* is a classic design Chesapeake Bay bugeye ketch built in Gloucester, Massachusetts, in 1964. She operates as a marine environmental education vessel sailing the waters of Long Island Sound from April through November.

Program type Sail training for crew and apprentices. Sea education in marine science and ecology in cooperation with accredited institutions. Dockside interpretation.

Specs Sparred length: 65'. LOA: 55'. LWL: 47'. Draft: 3'. Beam: 14'6". Rig height: 49'. Freeboard: 2'6". Sail area: 1,200 sq. ft. Tons: 14 grt. Hull: wood. Designer: Russell Grinnell. Built: 1964; Russell Grinnell, Gloucester, Mass. **Coast Guard cert.** Research vessel (Subchapter U). **Crew** 2-3. Trainees: 22. Age: 5+. Sex: co-ed. Dockside visitors: 25.

Contact Dr. Edwin Merritt, Executive Director, The Aquaculture Foundation, c/o Trumbull Public Schools, 6254 Main Street, Trumbull, CT 06611; 203 261-3801.

JOSEPH CONRAD

Former name *Georg Stage.* **Rig** ship, 3-masted. **Homeport/waters** Mystic, Conn.

Who sails? Individuals and organized groups ages 12 through 16. **Season** mid-June through August. **Cost** $75 per person per day; $67.50 at group rate.

Mystic Seaport's Sail Education Program offers young people the rare experience of living aboard the square-rigged ship *Joseph Conrad* as they learn sailing, seamanship, rowing, navigation and the arts of the sailor. The emphasis is on learning by doing and working together as a crew, while living aboard this famous ship, which is permanently berthed at Mystic Seaport Museum.

The *Joseph Conrad* program is open to individual boys and girls and organized groups ages 12 through 16. Applicants must have reached their twelfth birthday by January 1 of the year for which they are applying. Organized groups must have one adult leader per 10 participants. No prior experience is required for beginner sessions, only a desire to participate and learn. Intermediate sessions are for those who have attended a previous beginner session or have had sailing experience. All must hold current Red Cross swimmers certification or its equivalent.

Program type Sail training. Dockside visitation for school groups for elementary and high schools and individuals.

Specs Sparred length: 118'6". LOA: 100'8". Draft: 12'. Beam: 25'3". Rig height: 98'6". Tons: 213 grt. Hull: iron. Designer: Burmeister and Wain. Built: 1882; Burmeister & Wain, Copenhagen, Denmark. **Crew** 1 (day); 4 (overnight). Trainees: 54. Age: 12-16. Sex: co-ed.

Contact Dave Rayner, Museum Education Department, Mystic Seaport Museum, PO Box 6000, Mystic, CT 06355-0990; 860 572-0711; FAX 860 572-5328.

LADY MARYLAND

Rig pungy schooner (gaff rigged), 2-masted. **Homeport/waters** Baltimore, Md.: Chesapeake and Delaware Bays, East Coast between Maryland and Maine.

Who sails? Student and other organized groups, individuals and families. **Season** March through November. **Cost** $110 per person per day for overnight passages; $7,200 for 14 people for 5 days; $1,250 for day sail for 32 people.

Lady Maryland is an authentic pungy schooner, an elegant boat designed to haul cargo, fish, dredge for oysters, and carry luxury items quickly from port to port on Chesapeake Bay and along the Atlantic Coast. Instead of carrying watermelons and oysters, her mission today is to provide students with the opportunity to experience sailing an historic vessel while studying history, sailing, seamanship, marine science and ecology on her traditional waters from Maryland to Maine.

The Living Classrooms Foundation has developed a flexible educational program which can fit the needs of a variety of school and community groups. More than 30,000 students participate in LCF programs each year. The *Lady Maryland* operates educational day experiences for 32 passengers and extended live-aboard sail training and marine science programs for up to 14 people.

Program type Sail training with paying trainees. Sea education in marine science, maritime history and ecology for school groups from elementary school through colleges as well as adults.

Specs Sparred length: 104'. LOD: 72'. LWL: 64'3". Draft: 7'. Beam: 22'. Rig height: 85'. Freeboard: 3'. Sail area: 2,994 sq. ft. Tons: 60 grt. Power: twin 80 hp Cummins diesels. Designer: Thomas Gilmer. Built: 1986; G. Peter Boudreau, Baltimore, Md. **Coast Guard cert.** Passenger vessel (Subchapter T). **Crew** 6 (day); 8 (overnight). Trainees: 32 (day); 12-14 (overnight). Age: 13+. Sex: co-ed and single-sex cruises available. Dockside visitors: 40.

Contact Scott W. Raymond, Managing Director, Living Classrooms Foundation, The Lighthouse, Pier V, 717 Eastern Ave., Baltimore, MD 21202; 410 685-0295; FAX 410 752-8433.

LADY WASHINGTON

Rig brig. **Homeport/waters** Gray's Harbor, Wash.: Pacific Northwest.

Who sails? School groups from elementary school through college as well as individuals and families. Some trainees are placed through court referrals. Affiliated institutions include the Aberdeen, Wash. Public Development Authority. **Season** March to January. **Cost** Individual rates vary. $3,150 for full-day charter.

The brig *Lady Washington* was a consort to the *Columbia Rediviva*, the first American ship to circumnavigate the globe. The two ships left Boston for the lucrative fur trade of the Pacific Northwest on October 1, 1787. During the stormy passage around Cape Horn, the *Lady Washington,* under Captain Robert Gray, and Captain John Kendrick's *Columbia Rediviva* became separated. Gray arrived first at Nootka Sound on Vancouver Island, and after Kendrick arrived, they swapped ships and Kendrick engaged the *Lady Washington* in the fur trade with China. At Macao he had her re-rigged from a single-masted sloop to a two-masted brig, with both masts square rigged. The *Lady Washington* was the first flag flying the Stars and Stripes to visit Japan.

Built primarily of old-growth Douglas fir, the recreation of *Lady Washington* is the largest sailing replica built on the West Coast. The new vessel is as close to the original *Lady Washington* as historical records and U.S. Coast Guard regulations will allow. She is licensed as a passenger vessel and is also used for educational purposes.

Program type Sail training for crew, apprentices and paying trainees. Sea education in maritime history and ecology based on informal in-house programming. Passenger day sails and overnight passages. Dockside interpretation.

Specs Sparred length: 112'. LOA: 87'. LOD: 66'9". LWL: 58'. Draft: 11'. Beam: 24'. Rig height: 89'. Freeboard: 6'. Sail area: 4,400 sq. ft. Tons: 99'. Power: diesel. Hull: wood. Built: 1989; Aberdeen, Wash. Designer: Ray Wallace. Built: Grays Harbor Historical Seaport Authority. **Coast Guard cert.** Passenger vessel (Subchapter T). **Crew** 5. Trainees: 12. Age: 14+. Sex: co-ed.

Contact Les Bolton, Executive Director, Gray's Harbor Historical Seaport, PO Box 2019, Aberdeen, WA 98520; 206 532-8611.

LAND'S END

Rig ketch. **Homeport/waters** Newport, R.I.: Narragansett Bay, Rhode Island Sound and Long Island Sound.

Who sails? Individuals and groups. Affiliated institutions include Boy Scouts. **Season** March 15 to November 15.

Land's End was originally built for A. Lee Loomis, Jr., and Henry Loomis. She cruised to Bermuda in 1935 and then participated in the 1936 Bermuda Race. In 1939, the Loomises sailed *Land's End* from Seattle to Icy Bay, Alaska, and during World War II she remained on the West Coast. She returned to Boston's North Shore in 1947 under Henry Loomis's ownership. In 1992, *Land's End* was purchased by Robert Booth for use in youth programs and received an extensive refit. In 1995, *Land's End* was used for marine ecology programs for the Boy Scouts, and sail outreach programs for inner city and other youth oriented non-profit groups. She is operated by Square Sails School. Sail outreach is normally provided on a pay-as-you-can basis. It is typically provided free of charge to inner-city groups.

Program type Sail training for crew and apprentices provided as a resource for non-profit groups working with youth, including inner-city and drug rehabilitation programs. Sea education in marine science in cooperation with organized groups such as Boy Scouts.

Specs Sparred length: 49'. LOA: 39'3". LOD: 38'10". LWL: 35'. Draft: 6'. Beam: 10'10". Rig height: 55'. Freeboard: 5'7". Sail area: 868 sq. ft. Tons: 12 grt. Power: 37 hp inboard diesel. Hull: wood. Built: 1935; West Lynn, Mass. Designer: S. S. Crocker. Built: Britt Brothers. **Coast Guard cert.** Uninspected yacht. **Crew** 2. Trainees: 6 (day); 4 (overnight). Age: 10+. Sex: co-ed.

Contact Bob Booth, Square Sails School, 49 Bowen's Wharf, Newport, RI 02840; 401 847-7342.

LETTIE G. HOWARD

Former names *Caviare, Mystic C., Lettie G. Howard.* **Rig** gaff topsail schooner, 2-masted.
Homeport/waters New York City: New York Harbor, coastal New England

Who sails? School groups from elementary through college, individuals and families.
Affiliated institutions include PACE University.

The *Lettie G. Howard* is a *Fredonia*-model fishing schooner designed for fishing the Georges Banks in 1893 and built for Captain Fred Howard, of Beverly, Massachusetts, who named the schooner for his daughter. In 1901, the *Lettie G. Howard* was sold to E. E. Saunders and Co. in Pensacola, Florida, and she worked in the Gulf of Mexico fisheries until 1967. Briefly employed as a floating museum at Gloucester and named *Caviare*, in 1968 she was purchased by the South Street Seaport Museum and given back her original name.

After employing *Lettie G. Howard* as a floating exhibit for 20 years, in the late 1980s the museum decided that she should be restored to sailing condition. Today, she sails with a variety of curricula that focus on the history of the American fishing industry and related environmental issues, as well as sail training and general sea experience.

Program type Sail training. Sea education in maritime history and ecology.

Specs Sparred length: 125'4". LOA: 84'2". LOD: 78'7". LWL: 70'4". Draft: 10'6". Beam: 21'1". Rig height: 90'6". Freeboard: 3'5". Sail area: 5,072 sq. ft. Tons: 54 grt, 16 net, 11 disp. Power: twin Lugger diesels, twin screws. Hull: wood. Designer: George "Mel" McClain. Built: 1893; A. D. Story, Essex, Mass. (restored at South Street Seaport Museum in 1993). **Coast Guard cert.** Sailing school vessel (Subchapter R). **Crew** 6; 1 instructor. Trainees: 12 (overnight); 32 (day). Age: 12+. Sex: co-ed.

Contact Captain Michael Alden, Marine Education, South Street Seaport Museum, 207 Front St., New York, NY 10038; 212 748-8596.

LIBERTY

Former name *Schooner Liberty.* **Rig** gaff topsail schooner. **Homeport/waters** Boston, Mass. (summer), Key West, Fla. (winter): East Coast.

Who sails? School groups from elementary through high school, individuals and families. **Cost** $25 per person per 2-hour harbor cruise; $125 per person per day; $3,200 group rate charter per day.

Liberty is modeled on early 1800s coastal schooners used by New England fishermen and as cargo vessels. She is kept "shipshape and Bristol fashion" to meet the standards of our most discriminating clients. Boston's only Coast Guard-licensed tall ship carrying passengers for harbor cruises on a regular basis, *Liberty* is chartered to corporations, families and other groups for meetings, outings, client entertainment, weddings and other special events. *Liberty* travels to other New England ports for special maritime festivals. In addition, *Liberty* has created Tall Ship Theater with its production of *Harboring Boston's Mysteries*, a light-hearted history of Boston Harbor in the 18th and 19th-

centuries. Performed under sail by professional actors, the show features a revolutionary war battle, shipwrecks, mutinies hangings and a swashbuckling duel.

In the fall, *Liberty* makes the two-week passage to Key West with up to six passengers and begins a regular schedule of day sails, charters and Tall Ship Theater for the winter. Our Key West performance of *Shipwrecked* portrays Key West maritime history from the mid-1700s to 1920.

Program type Passenger day sails and overnight passages.

Specs Sparred length: 80'. LOA: 64'. LOD: 61'. LWL: 53'. Draft: 7'. Beam: 17'. Rig height: 65'. Freeboard: 5'. Sail area: 1,744 sq. ft. Tons: 50 grt. Power: diesel. Hull: steel. Designer: Charles Wittholz. Built: 1993; Treworgy Yachts, Palm Coast, Fla. **Coast Guard cert**. Passenger vessel (Subchapter T). **Crew** 3 (day); 4 (overnight). Trainees: 49 (day); 8 (overnight). Dockside visitors: 75.

Contact Gregory E. Muzzy, President, Schooner Liberty, Inc., 67 Long Wharf, Suite 1 North, Boston, MA 02110; 617 742-0333; FAX 617 742-1322.

LIBERTY CLIPPER

Former name *Mystic Clipper*. **Rig** gaff topsail schooner. **Homeport/waters** Boston, Mass.: East Coast. **Cost** $150 per person per day; $6,500 group rate charter per day.

Who sails? School groups from elementary through high school, individuals and families.

The *Liberty Clipper* is a replica of the mid-nineteenth-century Baltimore clippers, famous for their fast passage round Cape Horn on their way to California and Pacific ports. The schooner *Liberty Clipper* (formerly *Mystic Clipper*) joined *Liberty* in Boston in the summer of 1996. She will be available for charter to corporations, families and groups of up to 110 for day and evening Boston Harbor cruises. Her spacious decks and on-deck galley and bar create an ambiance under sail that will meet the expectation of our most discriminating client. As always, our guests are invited to join in hoisting the sails, steering the boat and otherwise joining in the fun. *Liberty Clipper* will also make several three- and five-day trips from Boston to other New England ports such as Provincetown, Martha's Vineyard and the Maine coast. The winter program will include a trip south and a southern itinerary.

Program type Passenger day sails and overnight passages.

Specs Sparred length: 125'. LOD: 86'. LWL: 76'. Draft: 8' (min.); 13' (max.). Beam: 25'. Rig height: 78'. Freeboard: 5'. Sail area: 4,300 sq. ft. Tons: 99 grt. Power: diesel. Hull: steel. Designer: Charles Wittholz. Built: 1983; Blount Marine Corp., Warren, R.I. **Coast Guard cert.** Passenger vessel (Subchapter T). **Crew** 5 (day); 10 (overnight). Trainees: 115 (day). Dockside visitors: 150.

Contact Gregory E. Muzzy, President, Schooner Liberty Clipper, Inc., 67 Long Wharf, Suite 1 North, Boston, MA 02110; 617 742-0333; FAX 617 742-1322.

LISA

Rig brig. **Homeport/waters** Wilmington, Del.: world wide. **Season** year round.

The brig *Lisa* offers teenagers the opportunity to sail before the mast in a new brig. Students can spend an academic year learning geography, history and math by direct experience, all while experiencing the disciplines of life at sea and the thrill of manning a traditional vessel.

Program type Full academic curriculum and special education programs for high school students and youth-at-risk.

Specs Sparred length: 72'. LOA: 55'. LWL: 45'. Draft: 6'3". Beam: 18'. Rig height: 55'. Freeboard: 5'. Sail area: 3,000 sq. ft. Tons: 40 grt. Hull: steel. **Coast Guard cert.** Uninspected yacht. **Crew** 4. Trainees: 6. Age: 13-19. Sex: co-ed.

Contact Captain John Leibolt, PO Box 16-1510, Altamonte Springs, FL 32716; 212 863-5718, 407 884-8333.

MABEL STEVENS

Rig ketch. **Homeport/waters** Cobb Island, Md.: Potomac River, Chesapeake Bay.

Who sails? Individuals and groups. **Season** April to October. **Cost** $70 per person per day; inquire for group rates.

The ketch *Mabel Stevens* offers a wide range of charter services in the Washington, D.C., and Chesapeake Bay areas. Sail training cruises, group and individual charters and other tailored sailing/maritime education programs are offered by Captain Chalker aboard the *Mabel Stevens*.

Built by Captain "Dick" Hartge of Galesville, Maryland, the *Mabel Stevens* holds a special place in the Washington metropolitan area. During the 1980s, the *Mabel Stevens* officially represented the District of Columbia at the tall ships events in Boston (350th anniversary) and New York (Statue of Liberty centennial) and in 1992 in New York at the Christopher Columbus Quincentennial Celebrations. Besides being the District of Columbia's goodwill ambassador vessel at major historic events, the *Mabel Stevens* competes in ASTA rallies and has in the past raced with the best of the Class C tall ships. In 1992, the *Mabel Stevens* was third in the tall ships race from Philadelphia to Newport; in 1986, she led the fleet of sail training vessels engaged in friendly competition en route to New York's Statue of Liberty festivities.

Program type Maritime history and environmental studies.

Specs Sparred length: 47'6". LOA: 35'. LWL: 31'9". Draft: 4'6". Beam: 11'6". Rig height: 45'. Freeboard: 3'. Sail area: 1,200 sq. ft. Sail no.: TS-US 159. Tons: 17 grt. Power: 52 hp diesel. Hull: wood. Built: 1935; Ernest H. Hartge, Galesville, Md. **Coast Guard cert.** Uninspected yacht. **Crew** 1. Trainees: 4. Age: all. Sex: co-ed and unisex cruises.

Contact Captain Ned Chalker, Ketch *Mabel Stevens*, 119 Fifth St., N.E., Washington, DC 20002; 202 543-0110, 301 259-4458; FAX 202 554-3949. E-mail: Nchalker@aol.com.

MADELINE

Rig gaff topsail schooner, 2-masted. **Homeport/waters** Lake Michigan.

Who sails? Members of the Maritime Heritage Alliance. *Madeline* is affiliated with the Association for Great Lakes History.

Madeline is a replica 1800s merchant schooner operated by the Maritime Heritage Alliance. She conducts regular sail training for Maritime Heritage Alliance members, and voyages to Great Lakes ports each summer.

Program type Sail training and maritime history for middle school, high school and adults.

Specs Sparred length: 92'. LOA: 55'6". LWL: 52'. Draft: 7'7". Beam: 16'2". Rig height: 65'. Freeboard: 2'2". Sail area: 2,200 sq. ft. Tons: 34 grt. **Coast Guard cert.** Uninspected yacht. **Crew** 4; 9 instructors. Trainees: 21 (day); 7 (overnight). Age: 12+. Sex: co-ed.

Contact Linda Strauss, Director of Operations, Maritime Heritage Alliance, PO Box 1108, Traverse City, MI 49685-1108; 616 946-2647.

MAHINA TIARE

Rig ketch. **Homeport/waters** Friday Harbor, Wash., and Auckland, New Zealand: South Pacific, coastal Chile and Antarctica.

Who sails? Blue water sailors. **Season** May to November (South Pacific), December-May (Chile and Antarctica).

Mahina Tiare has sailed approximately 9,000 miles per year as a sailing school vessel since 1990 in the North and South Pacific. Mahina Productions produces weekend Offshore Cruising Seminars geared for sailors who are considering or planning on making coastal or offshore passages on their own sailboats. Covered in these 20-hour exciting seminars are: boat selection; sail selection and repair; equipment and outfitting; cost of cruising; working while cruising; piloting and navigation; provisioning; women's point of view; anchoring techniques; weather and passage planning; cruising medicine; and safety equipment and practices. Presenters include authors John Neal and Barbara Marratt, sail maker Carol Hase, yacht designer Robert Perry and meteorologist Earl Seagars. John Neal and staff have presented 82 weekend Offshore Cruising Seminars since 1976 to over 4,500 students, many of whom have since circumnavigated the globe. The weekend seminar is included for students accepted on offshore sail-training legs aboard *Mahina Tiare*, which operates in the South Pacific.

Mahina Tiare 1996 and 1997 planned expeditions include voyages to Cape Horn, Antarctic, Patagonia, Alaska, Tahiti, and points beyond.

Program type Sail training with emphasis on navigation and ocean passages.

Specs LOA: 42'4". LWL: 34'5". Draft: 5'9". Beam: 12'5". Rig height: 55'1". Freeboard: 4'2". Sail area: 824 sq. ft. Sail no.: HR 42-70. Tons: 12 grt. Power: 62 hp Volvo diesel. Hull: fiberglass. Designer: Enderlien/Rassy. Built: 1993; Hallberg Rassy. **Crew** 1-2. Trainees: 4. Age: 30-70. Sex: co-ed.

Contact John Neal, *Mahina Tiare* Sailing Expeditions, PO Box 1696, Friday Harbor, WA 98250; 206 378-6131; FAX 206 378-4392.

MAINE

Rig Pinky schooner two-masted (gaff-rigged).

Homeport/waters Bath, Me.: coastal Maine and southern New England.

Maine was built by student apprentices at the Maine Maritime Academy between 1981 and 1985. She serves as a sail training ship for enrolled students and as a roving ambassador for the museum at special events.

Program type Sea education in maritime history.

Specs Sparred length: 56'. LOA: 43'. LOD: 40'. Draft: 8'. Beam: 12'. Freeboard: 2'6". Tons: 14 grt. Power: Westerbroke diesel. Hull: wood. Built: 1985; Maine Maritime Museum, Bath, Me.

Contact Kevin Johnson, Shipyard Supervisor, Maine Maritime Museum, 243 Washington St., Bath, ME 04530; 207 443-1316.

MALABAR

Former name *Rachel & Ebenezer.* **Rig** gaff topsail schooner, 2-masted. **Homeport/waters** Traverse City, Mich.: Great Lakes.

Who sails? Groups from middle schools and colleges, and individuals of all ages. Affiliated institutions include the Inland Seas Education Association. **Season** May to October.

Owned and operated by the Traverse Tall Ship Co., the schooner *Malabar* is one of the largest sailing vessels on the Great Lakes. She can accommodate 21 overnight guests and 47 passengers for day excursions. *Malabar* is fully certified by the U.S. Coast Guard. In conjunction with the Inland Seas Education Association, *Malabar* offers the Schoolship Program (spring and fall), an environmental, historical and sail training educational experience for junior high school students. The schooner also offers day sails, group charters and a popular floating bed and breakfast package.

Program type Sail training for crew and apprentices. Sea education in marine science and maritime history and ecology taught in cooperation with organized groups such as Scouts. Passenger day sails and overnight passages.

Specs Sparred length: 105'. LOD: 65'. LWL: 60'. Draft: 8'6". Beam: 21'. Rig height: 75'. Freeboard: 6'. Sail area: 3,000 sq. ft. Tons: 73 grt. Power: 136 hp diesel. Hull: ferro/steel. Designer: M. D. Lee. Built: 1975; Long Beach Shipyard, Bath, Me. **Coast Guard cert.** Passenger vessel (Subchapter T). **Crew** 6. Trainees: 40 (day); 21 (overnight). Age: 11-18. Sex: co-ed.

Contact Richard W. Budinger, President, Traverse Tall Ship Co., 13390 West Bay Shore Dr., Traverse City, MI 49684; 616 941-2000; FAX 616 941-0520.

MANITOU

Rig gaff topsail schooner, 2-masted. **Homeport/waters** Northport, Mich.: Great Lakes.

Who sails? School groups from middle school through college, individuals and families. Affiliated institutions include Eastern Michigan University. **Season** May to October.

Owned and operated by the Traverse Tall Ship Co., the schooner *Manitou* is one of the largest sailing vessels on the Great Lakes. She can accommodate 24 overnight guests and 60 passengers for day excursions. *Manitou* is fully certified by the U.S. Coast Guard and offers three-, five-, and six-day windjammer cruises into the northern parts of Lake Michigan, Lake Huron and the North Channel. In addition to her regular schedule, specialty passages are available to Beaver Island, Mackinac Island and the North

Channel. These include separate family packages for adventurous adults and their children. In conjunction with the Inland Seas Education Association, *Manitou* offers the "Schoolship" program (spring and fall), an environmental, historical and sail training educational experience for junior high school teachers and students.

Program type Sail training for crew and apprentices. Sea education in marine science, maritime history and ecology in cooperation with accredited high schools and other organized groups such as Scouts. Passenger day sails and overnight.

Specs Sparred length: 114'. LOD: 77'. LWL: 65'. Draft: 7' (min.); 11' (max.). Beam: 22'. Rig height: 80'. Freeboard: 6'. Sail area: 3,000 sq. ft. Tons: 82 grt. Power: 150 hp diesel. Hull: steel. Designer: Woodin & Marean. Built: 1982; Roger Gagnon Steel Ship Co., Portsmouth, N.H. **Coast Guard cert.** Passenger vessel (Subchapter T). **Crew** 6; 6 instructors. Trainees: 56 (day); 24 (overnight). Age: 12-60. Sex: co-ed.

Contact Richard W. Budinger, President, Traverse Tall Ship Co., 13390 West Bay Shore Dr., Traverse City, MI 49684; 616 941-2000; FAX 616 941-0520.

MARAMEL

Rig staysail schooner.

Homeport/waters Sausalito, Calif.: San Francisco Bay, Pacific Ocean. **Cost** $50 per person per day; $100 per person per day for overnight passages. $300 group rate; $500 group rate per day for overnight passages. Affiliated institutions include the Modern Sailing Academy.

Maramel has been active and well maintained during her 65 years. She is sea-kindly and able, having sailed extensively throughout the Atlantic and Pacific Oceans. In 1993, she successfully completed a 15,000-mile expedition from San Francisco to China via Micronesia and back by way of Japan and Alaska.

Her skipper, Captain Alan Olson, began teaching on the water at age 16. He enjoys introducing all ages to the sailing arts. Because of the small number of students (six maximum), teaching programs are flexible and the focus is on the particular needs and interests of the individual participants: from a day of simply appreciating sailing and learning the ropes, to coastal navigation and all the responsibilities of seamanship and navigation.

Program type Sail training for paying trainees. Sea education in maritime history and ecology in cooperation with such groups as Scouts. Passenger day sails and overnight passages. Dockside interpretation.

Specs Sparred length: 54'. LOA: 46'. LOD: 45'. LWL: 37'. Draft: 6'. Beam: 12'9". Rig height: 60'. Freeboard: 3'. Sail area: 1,300 sq. ft. Tons: 17 grt. Power: diesel. Hull: wood. Designer: William Hand. Built: 1929; Rankin & Richards, Seattle, Wash. **Crew** 2. Trainees: 6 (day); 4 (overnight). Dockside visitors: 15.

Contact Alan Olson, Captain/Owner, Schooner Expeditions, 300 Napa St., #26, Sausalito, CA 94965; 415 331-1282; FAX 415 242-1146. E-mail: LackeyAD@perkin-elmer.com.

MARTHA

Rig staysail schooner. **Homeport/waters** Seattle, WA: Pacific Northwest.

Who sails? High school through college age students, individuals and families. **Season** year round. **Cost** $100 per person per day. Group rate $600 per day.

The history of the nearly 90-year old *Martha* is quite remarkable, as few boats ever undergo the type of restoration she has experienced while being sailed worldwide under some three-dozen owners.

The 84 foot staysail schooner was built in 1907, rebuilt in 1968, and entirely re-built in 1976. Originally built for a San Francisco lumber executive and launched at the well-respected W. F. Stone Boatyard, her past includes a long racing career. In the late 1930s and early 40s *Martha* was owned by the actor, James Cagney, and then purchased by aluminum industrialist, Edgar Kaiser, in the 1960s. After moving her to the Northwest, Kaiser donated *Martha* to a youth camp on Orcas Island.

It was in the 1970s when the camp had her hauled to a shipyard in Seattle for maintenance work that the 50-ton yacht toppled from the boatyard cradle and was declared a total loss. But, she wasn't a total loss to Del Edgbert who purchased her and began a labor of love with his wife, Paulette. Their efforts resulted in a complete rebuild and restoration to her pre-1960 elegance, including the spectacular Honduran mahogany interior.

To prove her seaworthiness, Del also entered her in the 1979 Master Mariner's Race and cruised her to Alaska as well. The fruits of their labor were obvious when in 1981 *Martha* was virtually the best of the show at the Victoria Classic Boat Festival, winning best restoration, best sailboat, and oldest entry awards.

Martha is now the centerpiece of the Northwest Schooner Society, headquartered in Seattle, Washington. She is currently serving as a classroom for sailing students, an all-woman sail training program, and is available for naturalist sailing adventures in the spectacular San Juan Islands of Washington state. Come experience her magic!

Program Type Sail training for paying trainees — all-women sail training and Elderhostel programs. Maritime history, marine science and ecology of the beautiful North West.

Specs Sparred length: 84'. LOD: 67'. Draft: 7'. Beam: 16'. Freeboard: 4'. Sail area: 2,000 sq. ft. Tons: 30 grt. Power: 3-71 GMC diesel. Hull: wood. Designer: Crownshield. Built: 1907; W. F. Stone Boatyard, San Francisco, CA. **Crew** 2. Trainees: 6 for day and overnight programs..

Contact Karl Mehrer, President, Northwest Schooner Society, 1010 Valley Street, Seattle, WA 98109; 800 551-NWSS or 206 464-1973; E-mail: HTTP:\\ourworld.compuserv\com\homepages\deckweneh.

Mary Day

Rig gaff topsail schooner, 2-masted. **Homeport/waters** Camden, Me.: Mid-Coast and Downeast Maine.

Who sails? Individuals and families. **Season** May to October. **Cost** $100 per person per day.

Built in 1962 by Harvey Gamage, *Mary Day* combines the best aspects of the New England center-board coaster with modern design thinking. *Mary Day* operates out of Camden, Maine, in the windjammer trade from late May to early October. She carries 30 passengers on week-long vacation cruises in mid-coast Maine. *Mary Day* is a pure sailing vessel; she has no engine and depends on a small yawl boat when winds fail. She has a large and powerful rig and exhibits outstanding sailing abilities.

Mary Day carries a professional crew of six, including captain, mate, cook, two deck hands and one galley hand. The galley and one deck position are considered entry-level positions, and a great many sailing professionals have started out or gained valuable experience on board the schooner *Mary Day*.

Program type Sail training for crew and apprentices. Sea education in marine science based on informal, in-house programming. Passenger overnight passages. Dockside interpretation in homeport.

Specs Sparred length: 120'. LOA: 90'. LOD: 83'. Draft: 7'6". Beam: 22'. Rig height: 101'. Freeboard: 5'. Sail area: 5,000 sq. ft. Tons: 86 grt. Designer: H. Hawkins. Built: 1962; Harvey Gamage, South Bristol, Me. **Coast Guard cert.** Passenger vessel (Subchapter T). **Crew** 6. Trainees: 30 (day); 43 (overnight).

Contact Barry King, Camden Navigation Co., PO Box 798, Camden, ME 04843; 207 236-2750; E-mail: MaryDay@midcoast.com.

MIKE SEKUL

Rig gaff topsail schooner. **Homeport/waters** Biloxi, MS: coastwise Gulf of Mexico.

Who sails? Elementary students through college age, adults and families. Affiliated institutions include William Carey College. **Season** year round. **Cost** $15 per adult or $10 per child. (2 1/2 hour sail). Group rate (up to 49 people) $500 for 1/2 day, $750 per day.

The *Mike Sekul* is the second and newest of the two Biloxi oyster schooner replicas built as part of the Biloxi Schooner Project under the auspices of the Maritime and Seafood Industry Museum. She was launched in April of 1994 as part of the effort to preserve the maritime and seafood industry heritage of the Mississippi Gulf Coast. Money for construction and fitting out of the *Mike Sekul* and her sister ship, *Glenn L. Swetman*, has come from donations by interested individuals, businesses, civic groups, and a variety of museum-sponsored fund-raising events.

The *Mike Sekul* is available for charter for 2 1/2 hours, half-day, and full-day trips in the Mississippi Sound and to the barrier islands, Cat Island, Horn Island and Ship Island. Walk-up day sailing trips are made when she is not under charter. Groups of up to 49 passengers can learn about the maritime and seafood heritage of the Gulf Coast and about the vessels that were instrumental in Biloxi's seafood industry.

Sailing classes are offered through local college physical education departments and the museum's Sea and Sail Adventure summer camp. In addition she accommodates wedding parties, Elderhostel, and school groups.

Program Type Sail training for paying trainees, overnight trips to Horn Island, maritime history for elementary school students through adults, and children's (ages 6 - 13) Sea and Sail Adventure summer camp.

Specs Sparred length: 82'9". LOA: 78'. LOD: 50'. LWL: 47'. Draft: 5'10". Beam: 17'. Sail area: 2,499 sq. ft. Tons: 24 grt. Power: 4-71 Detroit diesel. Hull: wood. Designer: Traditional. Built: 1994; Neil Covacevich, Biloxi, MS. **Coast Guard cert.** Passenger vessel (Subchapter T). **Crew** 3. Trainees: 49 (day). Age: 15+. Sex: co-ed. Dockside visitors: 49.

Contact Robin Krohn, Manager, Maritime and Seafood Industry Museum, PO Box 1907, Biloxi, MS 39533; 601 435-6320; FAX 601 435-6309.

MINNIE V.

Rig skipjack sloop. **Homeport/waters** Baltimore, Md.: Baltimore Harbor.

Who sails? School groups from middle school through college as well as individuals and families. **Season** May through September.

Minnie V. is part of America's last fleet of working sail, dredging oysters from Chesapeake Bay in the winter and providing harbor tours and educational programs in the summer. Groups of young people hoist the sails and steer this classic vessel through the Old Port section of Baltimore for an unforgettable experience in social studies and ecology. History, economics and geography come to life as they observe the flow of national and world commerce through one of America's busiest seaports and discover landmarks that played key roles in American history — Fort McHenry, containership terminals, grain and coal docks, shipyards and manufacturing plants important to Baltimore's industrial life. Along the way, they learn something of the life of a sailor, the importance of the maritime world to their own lives, and the importance of keeping the waters clean. Teachers and group leaders

are supplied with packets of teaching exercises about maritime Baltimore in advance of the visit so that the group can make the most of this unique program.

Program type Sea education in marine science, maritime history and ecology in cooperation with accredited schools and colleges, and other organized groups. Passenger day sails. Dockside interpretation.

Specs Sparred length: 69'. LOD: 45'3". Draft: 3'. Beam: 15'7". Rig height: 58'. Freeboard: 2'. Sail area: 1,450 sq. ft. Tons: 10 grt. Power: yawl boat. Hull: wood. Built: 1906; Vetra, Wenona, Md. **Coast Guard cert.** Passenger vessel (Subchapter T). **Crew** 2. Trainees: 24. Age: all. Sex: co-ed. Dockside visitors: 24.

Contact Robert C. Keith, Program Director, Ocean World Institute, Inc., 831 South Bond St., Baltimore, MD 21231; 410 522-4214; FAX 410 732-3793.

MISTY ISLES

Rig gaff ketch. **Homeport/waters** Channel Islands, Calif.: Southern California.

Affiliated institutions include church youth groups. **Season** New Year's to Labor Day.

Misty Isles, a gaff-rigged ketch, whose motto is "Serving Fishers of Men," provides programs that are an outgrowth of years of experience with hands-on environmental education, Outward Bound programs, church youth group activities and mission outreach. *Misty Isles* conducts day and weekend sails in California waters from Morro Bay to San Diego. We train leaders through seamanship emphasizing teamwork, discipline, obedience, flexibility, self-reliance, judgment, moral and technical skills. A key long-range goal is to develop a shipboard program for adults to prepare for the GED test. Academic content will be integrated into *Misty Isles'* programs gradually. Marine/environmental studies will focus on the Channel Islands and coastal California. Her 1996 mission is with inner city and local church groups, introducing those served by these groups to sail training. The only cost for sailing aboard the *Misty Isles* is that of bringing your own food. Preparation and serving food underway is part of the teamwork, as is sail handling, navigating, anchoring and standing watches.

Program type Sail training for crew and apprentices.

Specs Sparred length: 60'. LOA: 50'. LOD: 49'. LWL: 44'. Draft: 9'. Beam: 12'. Rig height: 60'. Sail area: 1,500 sq. ft. Tons: 30 grt. Power: 80 hp Ford Lehman diesel. Hull: wood. Built: 1915. **Crew** 3 (day); 6 (overnight). Trainees: 20 (day); 12 (overnight).

Contact Ray Pike, Owner, P.O. Box 969, Key West, FL; 305 293-5458; FAX 305 293-5300.

MYSTIC WHALER

Rig gaff-rigged schooner. **Homeport/waters** Mystic, Conn.: southeast New England.

Who sails? School groups from elementary school through college, as well as individuals and families.

Built in 1967 for the New England windjammer trade, the *Mystic Whaler* is a tribute to the coastal trading schooners that plied her home waters a century ago. In 1990, after 23 years of service, the *Mystic Whaler* was retired. In 1994, John Eginton, a former captain of the *Mystic Whaler*, formed Mystic Whaler Cruises Inc., to purchase the hull and return the vessel to service. On June 10, 1995, after a thorough refit which included replacing the entire hull below the waterline the *Mystic Whaler* returned home to her dock on the Mystic River.

Program type Sail training for crew and apprentices. Sea education in maritime history and ecology based on informal programming with organized groups such as Scouts. Passenger day sails and overnight passages.

Specs Sparred length: 110'. LOA: 83'. LOD: 83'. LWL: 78'. Draft: 7'6" (min.); 13' (max.). Beam: 25'. Rig height: 90'. Freeboard: 7'. Sail area: 3,000 sq. ft. Tons: 97 grt. Power: 6-71 diesel, 175 hp. Hull: steel. Designer: "Chub" Crockett. Built: 1967; George Sutton, Tarpon Springs, Fla. **Coast Guard cert.** Passenger vessel (Subchapter T). **Crew** 5. Trainees: 65 (day); 36 (overnight). Dockside visitors: 65.

Contact Captain John Eginton, Mystic Whaler Cruises, Inc., PO Box 189, Mystic, CT 06355-0189; 203 536-4218; FAX: 203 536-4219.

NATALIE TODD

Rig gaff schooner, 3-masted. **Homeport/waters** Bar Harbor, Me.: coastal Maine.

Who sails? School groups from elementary school through college as well as individuals and families of all ages. **Season** May through mid-October.

The *Natalie Todd* spent the first four decades of her career as an offshore fishing vessel. Originally rigged as a two-masted "schooner-dragger," she made extended ground fishing trips to the Grand Banks and George's Banks. Modernized over the years, she eventually had her schooner rig removed, but continued fishing under power until 1986. In that year, the *Natalie Todd* was purchased by Captain Pagels and brought to Maine for a major rebuild and was re-rigged as a three-masted schooner. This gave her more sail than she had originally as a schooner-dragger, and also made the sail plan easier to handle by splitting it up into more manageable areas. Based in Bar Harbor, the *Natalie Todd* embarks on day sails along the coast of Acadia National Park, an especially spectacular part of the rock-bound Maine coast. Even on two-hour cruises, handling a 129-foot, three-masted schooner demands a high degree of concentration by trainees and makes for a very rewarding experience under sail.

Program type Sail training for apprentices and crew. Passenger day sails. Dockside interpretation.

Specs Sparred length: 129'. LOD: 101'. LWL: 89'. Draft: 10'. Beam: 21'. Rig height: 88'. Sail area: 3,900 sq. ft. Tons: 98 grt. Power: diesel. Hull: wood. Designer: Alan Woods. Built: 1941; Muller Boatworks, Brooklyn, N.Y. **Coast Guard cert.** Passenger vessel (Subchapter T). **Crew** 4. Trainees: 100. Sex: co-ed.

Contact Captain Steven F. Pagels, Downeast Windjammer Cruises, PO Box 8, Cherryfield, ME 04622; 207 546-2927; FAX 207 546-2023.

NATHANIEL BOWDITCH

Former names *Ladona, Jane Dore.* **Rig** topsail schooner, 2-masted. **Homeport/waters** Rockland, Me.: Maine coast.

Who sails? High school, college and special interest groups, individuals and families.

The schooner *Nathaniel Bowditch* is in her 20th year of operation carrying vacationing passengers on three-, four- and six-day cruises. Interspersed among her regularly scheduled cruises, which run from June through October, she frequently has carried groups from schools, colleges, summer camps and special interest groups. The *Bowditch* is a fine sailing vessel and raced often in her earlier years. During World War II she did a stint as a U.S. Coast Guard Offshore Picket Patrol, also known as the Hooligans Navy. Rebuilt in the 1970s and 1980s, the *Bowditch* now serves guests wishing to experience life and sailing on a traditional sailing vessel.

Program type Sea education in cooperation with accredited institutions. Passenger day sails and overnight passages. Dockside interpretation.

Specs Sparred length: 108'. LOA: 90'. LOD: 82'. Draft: 11'. Beam: 21'. Rig height: 92'. Sail area: 3,700 sq. ft. Tons: 54 grt. Power: 471 Detroit diesel. Hull: wood. Designer: William Hand. Built: 1922; Hodgdon Brothers, East Boothbay, Me. **Coast Guard cert**. Passenger vessel (Subchapter T). **Crew** 5. Trainees: 44 (day); 24 (overnight).

Contact G. E. Philbrick, Owner/Master, Schooner Nathaniel Bowditch of Cape Rozier, Inc., PO Box 459, Warren, ME 04864; 207 273-4062, 800 288-4098.

NEHEMIAH

Rig ketch. **Homeport/waters** Richmond, Calif.: San Francisco Bay and Pacific coast.

Who sails? Groups from elementary school through college and other organizations, individuals and families. Some trainees are court referred.

The sailing vessel *Nehemiah* and the non-profit Crosscurrent Voyages are the culmination of years of work by Captain Rod Phillips who has developed a program to use *Nehemiah* for the facilitation of personal growth and community involvement while challenging participants to learn and cooperate in an unfamiliar environment. Built using traditional shipbuilding techniques, she remains a fine example of expert craftsmanship and has proven her seaworthiness in two circumnavigations of the globe and extended cruising in the Pacific Ocean.

Crosscurrents Voyages' sailing trips can last from a few hours to a few days. Most are within the San Francisco Bay and Delta but qualified groups may choose to sail California coastal routes. Seamanship skills including navigation, line-handling, anchoring, galley management, oceanography and close observation of the marine environment and its sea life serve as a backdrop for the program structure. A wide variety of groups participate in the sail training program, including church leadership and youth groups, police activity leagues, youth-at-risk, sea scouts and school groups.

Program type Sail training for crew and apprentices. Sea education in marine science, maritime history and ecology. Passenger day sails and overnight passages. Dockside interpretation.

Specs Sparred length: 57'. LOA: 50'. LOD: 46'8". LWL: 39'. Draft: 6'. Beam: 14'3". Rig height: 58'. Freeboard: 5'. Tons: 23 grt. Power: Perkins 4-236. Hull: wood. Designer: William Garden (modified). Built: 1971; J. Meyr, Santa Barbara, Calif. **Coast Guard cert.** Passenger vessel (Subchapter T). **Crew** 2 (day); 4 (overnight). Trainees: 27 (day); 14 (overnight). Dockside visitors: 30.

Contact Captain Rod Phillips, Crosscurrent Voyages, 92 Seabreeze Dr., Richmond, CA 94804; 510 234-8202. E-mail: Compuserve.com76351.361.

NEW WAY

Former name *Western Union.* **Rig** gaff topsail schooner, 2-masted. **Homeport/waters** Philadelphia, Pa.: Atlantic Coast and Gulf of Mexico from Eastport, Me., to Brownsville, Tex.

Who sails? Participation is by reference from a cooperating agency. **Season** year round.

The *New Way* is one of two ships operated by VisionQuest, a non-profit organization that offers alternatives to conventional incarceration for troubled youth. Through VisionQuest's OceanQuest program, kids spend up to eight months at sea, learning the basic tenets of sailing, while receiving daily schooling and regular counseling. The challenges of life on board a sailing ship, combined with the guidance of VisionQuest's professional treatment staff, help the kids to recognize and overcome personal issues.

The ship's crew of 19 VisionQuest youths, 10 treatment staff and three maritime staff, spends five days a week at sea. The OceanQuest program has proven very effective in instilling a sense of self-discipline and respect for authority, while at the same time developing skilled crews. In 1992, VisionQuest's OceanQuest program was recognized by ASTA as the Sail Training Program of the Year.

Designed to lay and repair underwater telephone and telegraph cables in the seas off Key West, the *New Way* was acquired by VisionQuest in 1984.

Program type Sail training for crew and apprentices.

Specs Sparred length: 136'. LOA: 130'. LOD: 92'. LWL: 86'. Draft: 7'6". Beam: 23'. Rig height: 96'. Freeboard: 5'6". Sail area: 5,000 sq. ft. Tons: 91 grt. Power: twin 471 Detroit diesels. Hull: wood. Built: 1939; G. R. Steadman, Key West, Fla. **Coast Guard cert.** Passenger vessel (Subchapter T). **Crew** 3 (day); 6 (overnight). Trainees: 27 (day); 47 (overnight).

Contact Margaret Lannon, Program Master, VisionQuest National, Ltd., PO Box 447, Exton, PA 19341; 602 881-3950.

NIAGARA. U.S. BRIG

Rig brig. **Homeport/waters** Erie, Pa.: coastwise and Great Lakes.

Who sails? School groups from middle school through college, as well as individuals and families. **Cost** $15 for membership in the Flagship Niagara League.

On September 10, 1813, a small squadron of nine warships under the command of Commodore Oliver Hazard Perry defeated a British squadron of six ships near Put-In Bay. This naval engagement gave control of Lake Erie to the United States and forced the withdrawal of British forces that had invaded the Northwest Territory during the War of 1812. Perry's report of the victory — "We have met the enemy and they are ours..." — and his battle flag emblazoned with the legend "Don't give up the ship" are the best known remembrances of this battle. The present *Niagara* is a reconstruction built in 1988-90, and has auxiliary power and modern navigational equipment.

Niagara is inspected as an attraction vessel in port, and sails as an uninspected yacht. Her mission is to present living history, which in turn requires training of volunteer crew to sail the ship. *Niagara*'s typical schedule is two day sails per week and several weeks of voyaging to other ports for public visitation, usually a four-day passage and three days in port.

Program type Sail training for crew and apprentices. Sea education based on informal in-house programming. Dockside interpretation.

Specs Sparred length: 198'. LOA: 123'. LOD: 116'. LWL: 110'. Draft: 11'. Beam: 32'6". Rig height: 121'. Freeboard: 9'. Sail area: 12,600 sq. ft. Tons: 162 grt. Power: twin 180 hp diesels. Hull: wood. Designer: Melbourne Smith. Built: 1988; Erie, Pa. **Coast Guard cert.** Uninspected yacht and attraction vessel. **Crew** 40. Sex: co-ed. Dockside visitors: 200.

Contact Captain Walter P. Rybka, Pennsylvania Historical and Museum Commission, 164 East Front St., Erie, PA 16507; 814 871-4596, FAX 814 455-6760. E-mail: www.erie.net.

NINA

Rig caravel, 3-masted. **Homeport/waters** Corpus Christi, Tex.: Corpus Christi Bay.

Affiliated institutions Corpus Christi Museum of Science and History.

Niña, Pinta and *Santa Maria* are three replica ships built in Spain to commemorate the 500th anniversary of Christopher Columbus' voyage from Spain to the Bahamas in 1492. *Niña* is the only one to have been certified as a sailing school vessel. The three vessels are berthed adjacent to the Corpus Christi Museum of Science and History, which houses artifacts from one of the oldest known Spanish shipwrecks in the Americas. The museum also houses the Smithsonian Institution's "Seeds of Change" exhibit, which traces the impact of the European "discovery" on the indigenous peoples of the Americas and on Europe, including the exchange of flora, fauna, technology, and disease.

Program type Sail training for crew and apprentices. Sea education based on informal, in-house programming. Dockside interpretation at homeport.

Specs Sparred length: 92'8". LOA: 71'6". LOD: 64'. LWL: 59'. Draft: 7'. Beam: 21'. Rig height: 57'. Freeboard: 5'. Sail area: 1,507 sq. ft. Tons: 57 grt. Power: 3208 Caterpillar diesel. Hull: wood. Designer: Dr. José Maria Martinez Hidalgo, Barcelona Maritime Museum. Built: 1989; Cartagena Naval Shipyard, Spain. **Coast Guard cert**. Sailing school vessel (Subchapter R). **Crew** 3. Trainees: 15-20. Age: 14-70. Sex: co-ed. Dockside visitors: 90.

Contact David W. Hiott, Fleet Captain, Columbus Fleet Association, 1900 North Chaparral, Corpus Christi, TX 78401; 512 882-1260; FAX: 512 884-7392.

NORFOLK REBEL

Rig gaff schooner, 2-masted. **Homeport/waters** Norfolk, Va.: East Coast from Canada to the Gulf of Mexico. **Season** year round.

Captain Lane Briggs' "tugantine" is a favorite flagship for sail-assisted working vessels and is credited with a 1984 "circum-navigation of Virginia". The *Norfolk Rebel* is a familiar site to all involved in sail training and tall ships events up and down the Chesapeake.

Program type Sail training for crew and apprentices. Sea education in local maritime history and ecology based on informal, in-house programming. Dockside interpretation.

Specs Sparred length: 59'. LOA: 51'. LOD: 51'. LWL: 48'. Draft: 6'6". Beam: 15'3". Rig height: 50'. Freeboard: 4'6". Sail area: 1,700 sq. ft. Tons: 38 grt. Power: diesel. Hull: steel. Designer: Merritt N. Walter. Built: 1980; Howdy Bailey; Norfolk, Va. **Crew** 3 (day); 6 (overnight). Trainees: 3 (day).

Contact Captain Lane Briggs, Owner/Master, Rebel Marine Services, Inc., 1553 Bayville St., Norfolk, VA 23503; 804 588-6022; FAX 804 588-7102.

NORSEMAN

Rig Longboat. **Homeport/waters** Kalmar Shipyward, Wilmington, Del.: Chesapeake Bay, Delaware River, Jersey Shore, New York Bay and Hudson River.

Built in 1992, the Leif Ericson Viking Ship *Norseman* offers people a glimpse of Viking culture. With the crew dressed in full Viking regalia, the *Norseman* makes appearances at Scandinavian festivals and events from April through November. The highlight is the October 9 commemoration of Leif Ericson in Philadelphia.

Members and friends of the *Norseman* often gather to share their interests in Viking culture and Scandinavian heritage and to enhance their sailing and rowing skills. In the spring of 1996 the crew gathered at the Independence Seaport Museum to learn the fine art of making Viking ship oars.

The *Norseman* has participated in many sailing events in New York City as well as ports on the Hudson River, Long Island Sound and Delaware Bay. Because the *Norseman* is trailerable, she can be displayed either on her trailer or in the water. In 1995, the *Norseman* was filmed in the Greystone Productions documentaries "Biography: Leif Ericson" and "Ancient Mysteries: Vikings in North America," both of which have aired on the A&E cable channel.

Program type Sail training for crew and apprentices. Sea education in maritime history relevant to Viking period. Dockside interpretation.

Specs Sparred length: 40'. LOA: 36'. LOD: 32'. LWL: 30'. Draft: 3'. Beam: 9'. Rig height: 25'. Freeboard: 3'. Sail area: 297 sq. ft. Tons: 2 grt. Power: 25 hp outboard (mounted in well). Hull: fiberglass. Designer: Applecraft, Inc. Built: 1992; Applecraft, Inc. **Crew** 7-12. Trainees: 7-12. Dockside visitors: 18-20.

Contact Dennis Johnson, President, Leif Ericson Viking Ship, Inc., 511 East Mount Pleasant Ave., Philadelphia, PA 19119; 215 242-3063; FAX 215 242-3119. Captain David Segermark, 144 Ridgefield Rd., Newtown Square, PA 19073-3825; 610 356-3723; FAX 610 356-3758. E-mail: Viking@libertynet.org. Home page: http://Libertynet.org/~viking.

NORTHERN LIGHT

Rig 12-meter sloop. **Homeport/waters** Newport, R.I.: Narragansett Bay.

Who sails? Corporations who charter the vessels for team building and client entertaining.

A near sister ship of *Gleam*, the 12-meter *Northern Light* sank in Lake Michigan and was raised 12 years ago after which she underwent an extensive restoration before returning to Newport. Originally designed for America's Cup competition, the two boats now offer a unique team building program called "Your Own America's Cup Regatta." Each boat accommodates 13 guests plus three crew

members. No previous sailing experience is necessary to participate. Group and corporate outings are available in Newport, Rhode Island, and other New England ports.

Program type Sail training with paying trainees. Passenger day sails.

Specs Sparred length: 67'11". LOA: 67'11". LOD: 67'11". LWL: 46'11". Draft: 9'. Beam: 12'. Rig height: 90'. Freeboard: 3'. Sail area: 1,900 sq. ft. Tons: 30 grt. Power: aux. diesel. Hull: wood. Designer: Clinton Crane and Olin Stephens. Built: 1938; Henry Nevins, City Island, N.Y. **Coast Guard cert**. Passenger vessel (Subchapter T). **Crew** 3. Trainees: 14.

Contact Elizabeth Tiedemann, Director of Sales & Marketing, Seascope Systems, Inc., PO Box 119, 27 Rhode Island Ave., Newport, RI 02840; 401 847-5007; 401 849-6140.

Ocean Adventure

Rig schooner. **Homeport/waters** Tortola, British Virgin Is.: Caribbean (winter) and Ireland (summer).

Who sails? Adult trainees.

Ocean Adventure is a 60' schooner engaged in the crewed charter trade. In the winter she plies the waters of the Caribbean and in the summer she sails to and about Ireland and other European ports. In the Caribbean, although she is available for the traditional "sailing vacation," her main program is short-term (up to seven days) "blue water" adventure voyages, providing an opportunity for travelers to learn big boat sailing and handling, navigation and all the joys and rigors of open ocean sailing.

In June she sails to Ireland by way of Bermuda, a 30-day once-in-a-lifetime, never-to-be-forgotten ocean voyage. From July through September she sails port-to-port in Ireland and other European destinations. Come October, she returns to the Caribbean via the trade wind route stopping in Madeira and the Canaries.

Each program, under the guidance of experienced, certified ocean sailors, provides learning opportunities for the novice as well as the experienced sailor.

Program type Sail training with paying trainees on overnight passages.

Specs Sparred length: 60'. LOA: 56'. LWL: 47'. Draft: 9'. Beam: 15'. Rig height: 60'. Sail area: 1,232 sq. ft. Tons: 34.8 grt. Designer: G. Stead. Built: 1979; Southern Ocean Shipyard, Poole, England. **Crew** 2-3.

Contact Jack Callahan, Mid-Life Adventures, Ltd., 2513 West Peterson, Chicago, Ill. 60659; 800 621-8189; FAX 312 878-6355. E-mail: MidLifeAdv@aol.com.

OCEAN STAR

Rig schooner, 2-masted. **Homeport/waters** Portland, Me.: Atlantic, Caribbean and Gulf of Mexico.

Who sails? Adult trainees. **Season** year round.

The schooner *Ocean Star*, launched in 1991 as a navigation training vessel, has sailed over 76,000 blue water miles and trained over 500 adult students in the art and science of celestial navigation, coastal navigation, seamanship and marine weather. *Ocean Star* operates in Maine and Canadian waters during the summer and Caribbean/Gulf of Mexico in the winter. She makes frequent stops in Bermuda during her transits north and south.

Ocean Star sails professional crew which consists of a licensed captain, mate, cook and two deckhands. A staff instructor from *Ocean Navigator* magazine sails on each trip, providing personal and navigation instruction. In addition to attending classes during the day, trainees stand watch at night, assisting with navigation, steering and sail handling. Using traditional methods of navigation and relying on one-on-one instruction *Ocean Star* students learn to navigate by developing skills and using a range of equipment from sextants to radar, compass bearing and leadlines. Navigator Publishing, *Ocean Star*'s owner, produces *Ocean Navigator, Ocean Voyager* and *Professional Mariner* magazine.

Program type Sail training in navigation and seamanship, mostly offshore or near coastal waters.

Specs LOA: 88'. LOD: 73'. LWL: 65'. Draft: 9'. Beam: 20'. Rig height: 92'. Freeboard: 5'. Sail area: 4,600 sq. ft. Tons: 70 grt. Power: 210 hp diesel. Hull: steel. Designer: Bill Peterson. Built: 1991; Marine Metals, Norfolk, Va. **Crew** 7. Trainees: 6. Age: adults. Sex: co-ed.

Contact Gregory Walsh, *Ocean Navigator* Magazine, 18 Danforth St., Portland, ME 04101; 207 772-2466, 207 772-2879.

ODYSSEY

Rig ketch. **Homeport/waters** Key West, Fla. & San Diego, Calif.: global.

Who sails? High school and college students and adults.

Odyssey is owned and operated by the Whale Conservation Institute (WCI), a non-profit organization dedicated to preserving whales through ground-breaking research, education and conservation initiatives. Dr. Payne, President of WCI and internationally acclaimed marine scientist, is best known for his pioneering research on humpback whale songs and his unparalleled long-term research on the right whale. Under Dr. Payne's leadership, WCI has continually expanded the state-of-the-art in benign whale research techniques. The Institute combines rigorous science with a commitment to the welfare of whales and the ocean environment, and has helped people, regardless of their ideology, better understand and appreciate the natural world.

WCI's Global Ecotox Program, an assessment of the baseline levels of biopersistent toxins in the oceans, will be conducted from the *Odyssey*. We offer visiting scientist/student/donor/volunteer opportunities. In 1995 the *Odyssey* was featured in PBS's *New Explorers* series, Discovery Channel's *Finite Oceans*, BBC's *Paradise in Peril*, and in 1996, the IMAX production *Whale*.

Program type Sail training with paying volunteers and trainees. Sea education in cooperation with accredited schools and colleges in marine science, including marine mammal research, education and conservation programs. Overnight passages for major donors. Dockside interpretation during port visits.

Specs Sparred length: 94'. LOA: 85'. LOD: 85'. LWL: 69'. Draft: 11'. Beam: 18'6". Rig height: 89'. Freeboard: 6'. Sail area: 4,500 sq. ft. Tons: 100 grt. Power: Detroit diesel. Hull: steel. Designer: WECO/Whangarei. Built: 1976; WECO/Whangarei, New Zealand. **Crew** 4; 1 instructor. Trainees: 6.

Contact Iain Kerr, Director, Ocean Research Programs, Whale Conservation Institute, 191 Weston Rd., Lincoln, MA 01773; 617 259-0423; FAX: 617 259-0288.

ONTARIO, OMF

Rig topsail schooner. **Homeport/waters** Oswego, N.Y.: Great Lakes.

Who sails? School children, community groups and senior citizens.

On July 2, 1994, the hull of the schooner *OMF Ontario* was launched amidst the cheers of over 2,500 people from as far away as Florida and California. They came to see what a six-year commitment by an all-volunteer crew could do to stimulate interest and awareness in the Great Lakes. After two more years of fitting out with spars, rigging, sails, and

engine, the topsail schooner, built of welded steel to modern standards, will resemble many of the ships built at this location in the 19th-century. When complete, the schooner will serve as a "floating classroom" for the Education Through Involvement program which is designed to focus attention on the Great Lakes. Each lesson under sail will put participants of all ages through a "hands-on" experience of the history, heritage, resources and ecology of the Great Lakes. The program is intended to convey an understanding and appreciation of the role of the Great Lakes in our past, present and future.

Program type Passenger day sails for organized groups such as schools, community organizations and businesses. Dockside interpretation.

Specs Sparred length: 85'. LOA: 65'. LOD: 60'. Draft: 8'. Beam: 16'. Rig height: 70'. Freeboard: 6'. Sail area: 2,000 sq. ft. Tons: 42 grt. Power: 100 hp diesel. Hull: steel. Designer: Francis MacLachlan. Built: 1994; Oswego, N.Y. **Coast Guard cert**. Passenger vessel (Subchapter T). **Crew** 2; 4 instructors. Trainees: 25. Dockside visitors: 40.

Contact Richard Pfund, Director, Oswego Maritime Foundation, 41 Lake St., Oswego, NY 13126; 315 342-5753.

PACIFIC SWIFT

Rig square topsail schooner, 2-masted. **Homeport/waters** Victoria, B.C.: Pacific Northwest, North and South Pacific, Caribbean and Atlantic.

Who sails? Individuals and groups. **Season** year round. **Cost** Can $55 per day per trainee.

Pacific Swift, a 111' topsail schooner modeled on the brig *Swift* of 1778, was built at Expo '86 in Vancouver, British Columbia, as a working exhibit at the World's Fair. Since her completion in 1988, she has sailed over 68,000 deep-sea miles, crossing both the Pacific and Atlantic twice in the course of her offshore sail training programs. During the summer months she usually returns to the Pacific Northwest, where she sails on 10-day trips with SALTS' other training ship, the Grand Banks schooner *Robertson II.*

Both vessels take over a thousand young people to sea each year. These teenagers participate in all facets of shipboard life, from bosun's chores to helmsmanship, with formal instruction in navigation, pilotage, seamanship and small boat handling. Rooted in Christian values, SALTS believes that training under sail provides the human spirit a real chance to develop and mature.

Program type Maritime history and nautical instruction.

Specs Sparred length: 111'. LOA: 83'. LOD: 78'. LWL: 65'. Draft: 10'8". Beam: 20'6". Rig height: 92'. Freeboard: 3'6". Sail area: 4,111 sq. ft. Tons: 98 grt. Power: Isuzu diesel 220 hp. Hull: wood. Designer: traditional. Built: 1986; SALTS, Vancouver, British Columbia. **Coast Guard cert.** Canadian passenger vessel; sail training vessel. **Crew** 5. Trainees: 30. Age: 13-25. Sex: co-ed.

Contact Captain Martyn J. Clark, Executive Director, Sail and Life Training Society (S.A.L.T.S.), Box 5014, Station B, Victoria, British Columbia V8R 6N3 Canada; 604 383-6811; FAX 604 383-7781.

PALAWAN

Rig cutter. **Homeport/waters** Portland, Me.: Casco Bay, Caribbean.

Who sails? Students, adults and groups. **Cost** $125 per person per day; $950 group rate.

Designed and built in 1965 as an ocean racer under the old Cruising Club of America rule, *Palawan* achieved a number of firsts. An early aluminum yacht, she was the first off-shore boat to use the fin-keel. Although she could not keep up with the newer hulls encouraged by the IOR rule, everyone spoke highly of the boat, and designer Olin Stephens declared her "perhaps the easiest steering boat I ever drew." Her racing career has been an active one, and she was used by the Maine Maritime Academy for over 10 years as a training vessel — a long time for a donated boat!

Palawan has operated as a passenger vessel since 1988 in Portland, Maine, serving both individuals and groups, and she is a popular vehicle for fund-raising events such as Friends of Casco Bay, Maine Island Trails and others. A winter season may be spent as a yacht in warmer waters with up to six crew aboard.

Program type Sail training with team-building activities for paying trainees. Passenger day sails and overnight passages.

Specs Sparred length: 58'. LOA: 58'. LOD: 58'. LWL: 40'. Draft: 8'1". Beam: 12'4". Rig height: 68'. Freeboard: 4'4". Sail area: 1,308 sq. ft. Tons: 24 grt. Power: 60 hp aux. Hull: aluminum. Designer: Olin Stephens. Built: 1965; Derecktor, New York. **Coast Guard cert**. Passenger vessel (Subchapter T). **Crew** 2 (day); 3 (overnight). Trainees: 24 (day); 6 (overnight).

Contact Captain Tom Woodruff, Palawan Services, Inc., PO Box 9715-240, Portland, ME 04104; 207 773-2163; FAX 207 781-5530.

PICARA

Rig sloop. **Homeport/waters** Orleans, Mass.: Atlantic Coast between New York and Canada.

Who sails? Sea Explorers and other groups. **Affiliated institutions** Sea Explorers, BSA.

The Nauset Sea Explorer group celebrates more than 40 years of sail training. This program teaches seamanship and sailing to young people between the ages of 14 and 20 through education and annual cruises along the New England Coast. While on extended cruises, each scout takes part in every aspect of the voyage, from cooking and planning meals to navigation and sail repair, to actually sailing the boat. The group has chartered for a week-long cruise in the

Virgin Islands each winter, and undertakes summer cruises along the New England Coast. They also operate two 17' sailboats and a 21' Boston Whaler. They have participated in such tall ships gatherings as the New York World's Fair 1964, Montreal's Expo '67, OpSail '76 for the nation's bicentennial, Boston's 350th anniversary in 1980, and the culminating events of the Grand Regatta 1992 Columbus Quincentenary in both New York and Boston.

Program type Sail training for crew and apprentices. Sea education with Sea Scouts. Passenger day sails and overnight passages. Dockside interpretation during outport visits.

Specs Sparred length: 36'. LOA: 36'. LWL: 28'. Draft: 5'6". Beam: 12'. Rig height: 49'. Freeboard: 4'. Sail area: 750 sq. ft. Tons: 15 grt. Power: 4,108 Perkins diesel. Hull: fiberglass. Designer: S-2 Yachts. Built: 1982; S-2 Yachts, Holland, Mich. **Coast Guard cert.** Uninspected yacht. **Crew** 2. Trainees: 20 (day); 11 (overnight). Age: 14-20. Sex: co-ed.

Contact Captain Michael F. Allard, Nauset Sea Explorers, Boy Scouts of America, , PO Box 1236, Orleans, MA 02653; 508 255-5260.

PILGRIM

Rig snow/brig. **Homeport/waters** Dana Point, Calif.: Point Conception to Ensanada, Mexico. **Season** year round.

Who sails? Student groups and individual volunteers.

The *Pilgrim* is a full-scale replica of the ship immortalized by Richard Henry Dana in his classic *Two Years Before the Mast.* Owned and operated by the Orange County Marine Institute, *Pilgrim* is dedicated to multi-disciplinary education. During the school year, the Marine Institute offers an 18-hour-long, award-winning living history program that offers a hands-on exploration of literature, California history and group problem solving in which crew members re-create the challenge of shipboard life. Students re-live the life of a sailor of the 1830s as they hoist barrels, row in the harbor, stand night watches, swab the decks and learn to cope with a stern captain.

On summer evenings, audiences are treated to the sights and sounds of the sea as the *Pilgrim*'s decks come alive with theatrical and musical performances. In late summer the *Pilgrim* sails on her annual cruise with an all-volunteer crew to ports along the California coast as a goodwill ambassador for the City of Dana Point. She returns in September to lead the annual Tallship Parade and Festival.

Program type Maritime history and environmental studies for youth at risk.

Specs Sparred length: 130'. LOD: 98'. Draft: 9'. Beam: 24'6". Rig height: 104'. Freeboard: 8'. Sail area: 7,600 sq. ft. Tons: 99 grt. Power: diesel. Hull: wood. Designer: Ray Wallace. Built: 1945; A, Nielsen, Holbaek, Denmark. **Coast Guard cert.** Uninspected yacht. **Crew** 35. Dockside visitors: 50.

Contact Daniel Stetson, Director of Maritime Affairs, Orange County Marine Institute, 24200 Dana Point Harbor Drive, Dana Point, CA 92629; 714 496-2274; 714 496-4296.

PILGRIM

Rig square topsail schooner. **Homeport/waters** Lake Ontario and St. Lawrence River.

Who sails? Individuals and student groups. **Season** May to October.

The *Pilgrim* sails primarily the waters of Lake Ontario and the Thousand Islands area of the St. Lawrence River. This schooner's main mission lies in creating an interest and appreciation of our Great Lakes maritime heritage and environment. The *Pilgrim* offers varied curricula, private charters and participation in historical reenactments.

The captain and crew seek to instill in their students the importance of responsibility, leadership and teamwork. We welcome the challenge of fulfilling the dreams of would-be sailors through unique hands-on opportunities designed especially for you and your group.

Program type Maritime history, nautical science, private charters, historical reenactments.

Specs Sparred length: 68'. LOA: 68'. LOD: 52'. LWL: 44'3". Draft: 6'. Beam: 15'. Rig height: 57'. Freeboard: 3'6". Sail area: 2,500 sq. ft. Tons: 33 grt. Power: 85 hp diesel. Hull: steel. Designer: Wood. Built: 1987; Marine Metals. **Coast Guard cert.** Uninspected yacht. **Crew** 2. Trainees: 6. Sex: co-ed.

Contact Captain Gary Kurtz, Schooner *Pilgrim*, Pilgrim Packet Co., PO Box 491, Kendall, NY 14476; 716 682-4757.

PIONEER

Rig gaff schooner, 2-masted. **Homeport/waters** New York, N.Y.: New York Harbor, Hudson River and Atlantic coast.

Who sails? Affiliated institutions include the New York City public school system and area private schools. **Season** spring, summer and fall. **Cost** $250 per 90-minute group program.

The first iron sloop built in the United States, *Pioneer* is the only surviving American iron-hulled sailing vessel. Her long career included 10 years hauling sand for an iron foundry in Chester, Pennsylvania, freighting bulk cargoes such as coal, lumber and oil, and work with a marine contracting company. She was given a schooner rig in 1895 and given an engine in 1903. In 1966, Gloucester dock builder Russell Grinnell, Jr., restored her to use as a functional working schooner and used *Pioneer* in his dock building business until his death in 1970; shortly thereafter, she was donated to the South Street Seaport Museum.

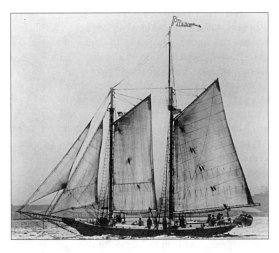

First employed to carry drug rehabilitation patients on voyages along the New England coast, *Pioneer* is now dedicated to recreating nineteenth-century sailing for the public. Carrying a crew of professionals and volunteers, she offers public sails, private charters, programs for the handicapped and school programs in the waters of New York Harbor. She generally heads south in the fall to sail the Delaware and Chesapeake Bays.

Program type Sea education in maritime history. Special education programs for middle- and high-school students.

Specs Sparred length: 102'. LOA: 64'5". LWL: 58'11". Draft: 4'8" (min.); 12' (max.). Beam: 21'6". Rig height: 56'6"; 76' with topmast. Freeboard: 3'. Sail area: 2,700 sq. ft. Tons: 43 grt. Power: 135 hp diesel. Hull: originally iron, replated in steel. Built: 1885; Pioneer Iron Co., Marcus Hook, N.J. (rebuilt 1968; Somerset, Mass.). **Coast Guard cert.** Passenger vessel (Subchapter T). **Crew** 4-12; 2 instructors. Trainees: 40 (day). Age: 7-18+. Sex: co-ed.

Contact Captain Zack Thomas, South Street Seaport Museum, 207 Front St., New York, NY 10038; 212 748-8684.

PRIDE OF BALTIMORE II

Rig square topsail schooner, 2-masted. **Homeport/waters** Baltimore, Md.: world wide.

Who sails? Affiliated institutions include the State of Maryland, City of Baltimore. **Season** year round. **Cost** $150 per person per day. $500 group rate per hour (dockside); $750 group rate per hour (sailing).

The *Pride of Baltimore II* is a topsail schooner built to the lines of an 1812-era Baltimore Clipper. Owned by the State of Maryland and operated by Pride of Baltimore, Inc., her primary mission is to promote tourism and economic development for the Maryland and the Port of Baltimore worldwide. *Pride of Baltimore II* is available for charter and for dockside and sailing receptions anywhere on her schedule, and she can accommodate up to six paying passengers for hire between ports of call.

The *Pride of Baltimore II* sails year round with two full-time rotating captains and a crew of 11. Preference in hiring for the crew of 11 is given to Maryland residents. The *Pride of Baltimore II* maintains an international sailing schedule, and most recently has visited South America, the U.S. West Coast and in the summer of 1996 she toured Europe.

Program type Sea education in cooperation with accredited schools and colleges. Passenger day sails and overnight passages. Dockside interpretation.

Specs Sparred length: 170'. LOA: 108'. LOD: 96'6". Draft: 12'4". Beam: 26'. Rig height: 107'. Freeboard: 6'. Sail area: 10,442 sq. ft. Tons: 97 grt. Power: twin 165 hp Caterpillar diesels. Hull: wood. Designer: Thomas C. Gillmer. Built: 1988; G. Peter Boudreau, Baltimore, Md. **Coast Guard cert.** Passenger vessel (Subchapter T). **Crew** 12. Trainees: 35 (day); 6 (overnight). Age: 18+. Sex: co-ed. Dockside visitors: 107.

Contact W. Bruce Quackenbush, Jr., Executive Director, Pride of Baltimore, Inc., 401 East Pratt St., Baltimore, MD 21202; 410 539-1151; FAX 410 539-1190.

PROVIDENCE

Rig square topsail sloop. **Homeport/waters** Newport, R.I.: Atlantic Ocean and Great Lakes.

Who sails? Individuals, students and other groups. Affiliated institutions include Sea Explorer Ship 76.

Providence is a full-sized replica of John Paul Jones's first command, the ex-merchant vessel *Katy*, the first ship commissioned by the Continental Navy. The original *Providence* carried 12 guns and was so successful in her campaign against the British — all told she sank or captured 40 ships — that she became known as the "Lucky Sloop." Jones made his first command famous and said of her, "She was the first, and she was the best." Under subsequent captains, *Providence* became the first ship to land U.S. Marines and to fly the American flag on foreign soil.

The non-profit Seaport '76 built the replica *Providence* in celebration of the U.S. Bicentennial and to stimulate interest in our country's early maritime heritage. She has logged more than 200 port calls to more than 100 different cities as she carries out her educational mission. Individuals interested in joining the *Providence* as apprentices are welcome year-round. The ship is available for charter underway and at dockside, for education, special events, documentary and film use, and historic reenactments.

Program type Maritime history for youth-at-risk, middle- and high school students and adults. Commercial chartering.

Specs Sparred length: 110'. LOA: 66'7". LWL: 59'. Draft: 10'. Beam: 20'. Rig height: 94'. Freeboard: 8'. Sail area: 3,470 sq. ft. Tons: 68 grt. Power: 170 hp diesel. Hull: fiberglass and wood. Designer: Charles W. Wittholz. Built: 1976; Seaport '76 Foundation, Melville, R.I. **Coast Guard cert.** Passenger vessel (Subchapter T). **Crew** 7-10. Trainees: 24-40 (day); 7 (overnight). Sex: co-ed.

Contact Ruth Taylor, Rhode Island Historical Society, 110 Benevolent St., Providence, RI 02906; 401 331-8578 x125; FAX 401 351-0127. E-mail: SloopProv@aol.com.

QUINNIPIACK

Former name *Janet May*. **Rig** gaff schooner, 2-masted. **Homeport/waters** New Haven, Conn.: Long Island Sound.

Who sails? Student groups and individuals. Affiliated institutions include various public and private elementary and high schools. **Season** April to November.

Founded in 1975, Schooner, Inc., provides educational opportunities in environmental marine sciences aboard their 91' wooden schooner, *Quinnipiack*. Students of all ages and abilities participate in science studies under sail exploring the biology and ecology of Long Island Sound while experiencing a taste of our maritime heritage. Shipboard programs with Schooner Inc.'s marine biologist complement traditional classroom studies in many sub-

ject areas. While the emphasis of the program is on biology and ecology, aspects of geography, history, chemistry and navigation are covered. At the interactive learning stations aboard *Quinnipiack*, students look at plankton through microscopes, trawl for marine life, perform water chemistry tests and conduct land-use surveys. The subject matter and level of instruction are tailored to the needs of the group. The "Mates Program" gives high school youths an opportunity to learn how to sail a traditional schooner while serving as volunteer crew members. Our co-ed staff includes a USCG-licensed captain, a marine biologist and trained crew.

Program type Sail training for crew, apprentices and trainees. Sea education in marine science, maritime history and ecology in cooperation with accredited schools and colleges.

Specs Sparred length: 92'. LOA: 72'. LOD: 65'. LWL: 58'. Draft: 4'6" (min.); -8'6" (max.). Beam: 20'. Rig height: 62'. Freeboard: 5'. Sail area: 2,400 sq. ft. Tons: 41 grt. Hull: wood. Designer: Phil Sheldon. Built: 1984; Phil Sheldon, Milbridge Maine. **Coast Guard cert.** Passenger vessel (Subchapter T). **Crew** 4. Trainees: 40. Age: 12-18. Sex: co-ed. Dockside visitors: 52.

Contact Captain Bob Boulware/Karl Rosenbaum, Executive Director, Schooner, Inc., 60 South Water St., New Haven, CT 06519; 203 865-1737; FAX 203 624-8816.

ROSE, HMS

Rig full-rigged ship, 3-masted. **Homeport/waters** Bridgeport, Conn.: East Coast (summer); overseas.

Who sails? Individuals and groups of all ages. **Season** year round. **Cost** $110 per person per day.

The full-rigged ship "HMS" *Rose* was built in 1970, patterned and named after the Royal Navy's sixth-rate HMS *Rose*, a 24-gun ship built in 1757. During the French and Indian War, when George Washington wore the red coat of a commissioned British officer, HMS *Rose* was stationed in the Caribbean. In 1984, the "HMS" *Rose* was purchased by the "HMS" Rose Foundation and since 1985 she has been entirely rebuilt to meet or exceed all safety requirements for a vessel of her class and size.

The largest vessel certified as a sailing school vessel by the U.S. Coast Guard, *Rose* can embark 100 people for day sails and 49 people for overnight passages. Sail training passages along the east coast, the Great Lakes and even to Europe last from a day to as much as several months. Special one-day programs are often scheduled for corporate, civic or other groups.

Program type Maritime history, environmental studies for middle school and high school students and corporate team building programs for adults.

Specs Sparred length: 179'. LOA: 135'. LOD: 125'. LWL: 105'. Draft: 13'. Beam: 32'. Rig height: 130'. Freeboard: 13'. Sail area: 13,000 sq. ft. Tons: 500 grt. Power: twin diesels. Hull: wood. Designer: original design by Hugh Blades, British Admiralty, in 1757, revised by Phil Bolger. Built: 1969/70; Smith & Rhuland, Lunenberg, N.S. (rebuilt: 1985-87; Bridgeport, Conn. and Fairhaven, Mass.). **Coast Guard cert.** Sailing school vessel (Subchapter R) and attraction vessel. **Crew** 18. Trainees: 85 (day); 31 (overnight). Age: junior high school to adult. Sex: co-ed.

Contact "HMS" Rose Foundation, Inc., One Bostwick Ave., Bridgeport, Conn. 06605; 203 335-0932, 203 335-1433; FAX 203 335-6793.

ST. LAWRENCE II

Rig brigantine. **Homeport/waters** Kingston, Ont.: Lake Ontario and adjacent waters.

Who sails? Elementary school groups and Sea Cadets. **Season** April to November (sailing); October to March (winter program). **Cost** Can $45 per person per day; Can $1,200 per day group rate.

The STV *St. Lawrence II* is a purpose-built sail training vessel that has operated, primarily on the Great Lakes, since 1956. Her owners believe that hard work and responsibility at a young age creates better citizens. Her complement of 29 comprises 18 new trainees, three petty officers, bosun's mate, bosun, chef, three watch officers, and an executive officer, all between the ages of 13 and 18. The

captain is the only adult aboard. Trainees in this hands-on program are encouraged to learn by doing, and progress is monitored by the Canadian Sail Training Association grade standards. Officers are graduates of Brigantine, Inc.'s, winter training program, which includes lectures on seamanship, navigation and safety and ship's systems, as well as maintenance of the ship. Every year *St. Lawrence* sails over 4,000 miles, spends more than 40 nights at sea and introduces 150 trainees to the rigors of life aboard ship on the Great Lakes. Brigantine, Inc., also has a lead-up program for 11- to 13-year-olds providing three-day cruises on Lake Ontario and the St. Lawrence River.

Program type Sail training with paying trainees.

Specs Sparred length: 72'. LOA: 60'. LOD: 57'. LWL: 46'. Draft: 8'. Beam: 15'. Rig height: 54'. Freeboard: 4'6". Sail area: 2,560 sq. ft. Tons: 34 grt. Power: 165 hp diesel. Hull: steel. Designer: Francis A. MacLachlan. Built: 1955; Kingston Shipyards, Kingston, Ont. Trainees: 29 (day); 18 (overnight). Age: 13-18 (sometimes 11-adult). Sex: co-ed.

Contact Gordon Workman, Manager, Brigantine, Inc., 53 Yonge St., Kingston, Ontario K7M 6G4 Canada; 613 544-5175; FAX 613 544-5175.

SEA LION

Rig bark. **Homeport/waters** Buffalo, N.Y: Lakes Erie and Ontario.

Who sails? School groups from elementary school through college, individuals and families. Affiliated institutions include Buffalo State College and Medaille College.

The *Sea Lion* is a 62' 17th-century English merchant vessel fashioned after the *Mayflower II*. Constructed on Chautauqua Lake, New York, using only those tools and techniques that would have been available in the mid-1600s, the ship is considered one of the most accurate reproductions of its kind in the United States.

The Buffalo Maritime Society, an all volunteer not-for-profit corporation, acquired and moved the *Sea Lion* to Buffalo in 1992. Since then renovations have been underway to prepare her for use as a "living platform for education." *Sea Lion* will cruise the waters of Lake Erie and Lake Ontario. She will be open for tours and her crew will offer free classes in maritime history, navigation skills and environmental issues. Sail training courses for volunteers interested in crewing are also available. Other activities include theater, music, literary programs and art appreciation.

Program type Sail training for crew and apprentices. Sea education in marine science, maritime history and ecology based on informal in-house programming in cooperation with accredited schools and other groups. Dockside interpretation.

Specs Sparred length: 65'. LOA: 53'. LOD: 50'. LWL: 42'. Draft: 6'6". Beam: 13'. Rig height: 52'. Freeboard: 6'. Sail area: 1,300 sq. ft. Tons: 48 grt. Power: none. Hull: wood. Designer: William A. Baker. Built: 1986; Sea Lion Project, Chautauqua, N.Y. **Coast Guard cert**. Attraction vessel. Trainees: 15. Dockside visitors: 20.

Contact Timothy Downey, President, Buffalo Maritime Society, Inc., 90 Liberty Terrace, Buffalo, NY 14215; 716 648-3936, 716 834-3922; FAX 716 834-0149.

SHENANDOAH

Rig square topsail schooner, 2-masted. **Homeport/waters** Martha's Vineyard, Mass.: Long Island to Nantucket.

Who sails? Paying passengers. **Season** June to September. **Cost** $75 per person per day; group rates (30 people for six days): $12,000 (June and September), $15,000 (July and August).

While the *Shenandoah* is not a replica, the vessel's design bears a strong resemblance to that of the U.S. Revenue Cutter *Joe Lane* of 1851. For her first 25 years, the rakish square topsail schooner was painted white, but she now wears the black and white checker-board paint scheme of the 19th-century Revenue Service. Every summer *Shenandoah* plies the waters of southern New England and Long Island Sound visiting the haunts of pirates and the homeports of whaling ships. *Shenandoah*'s economic bottom line is paying passengers. That reality includes sharing one's world with the weekly passengers, which can be a satisfying and sometimes challenging endeavor.

Program type Sail training and windjammer cruises with paying passengers.

Specs Sparred length: 152'. LOA: 108'. LWL: 101'. Draft: 11'. Beam: 23'. Rig height: 94'. Freeboard: 3' (amidships). Sail area: 7,000 sq. ft. Tons: 85 grt. **Coast Guard cert.** Passenger vessel (Subchapter T). **Crew** 9. Trainees: 35 (day); 30 (overnight). Age: 12-20. Sex: unisex.

Contact Captain Robert S. Douglas, Coastwise Packet Co., Inc., PO Box 429, Vineyard Haven, MA 02568; 508 693-1699.

SOUNDWATERS

Rig three-masted sharpie (gaff schooner). **Homeport/waters** Stamford, Conn.: Long Island Sound.

Who sails? School and other groups. **Season** April to November. **Cost** $25 per person per day. $600-$1,500 group rate.

SoundWaters is a non-profit environmental organization dedicated to the restoration and preservation of Long Island Sound. Sailing port-to-port in Connecticut and Westchester County and Long Island, New York, the *SoundWaters* offers a multi-disciplinary education program that introduces adults and children to the ecological wonders of Long Island Sound. The eco-story curriculum integrates Long Island and environmental concerns into history, social science, mathematics and language arts lessons. (Graduate-credit courses are available for educators).

SoundWaters' Eagle mariner program offers summer sail training and marine ecology of Long Island Sound aboard *SoundWaters*. One-week day and overnight sessions are scheduled in July and August for 11- to 14-year-olds. The program includes instruction in basic seamanship and ship handling; navigation and nautical knots; weather forecasting and marine ecology. Field experience may include exploring a salt marsh, sailing to a local lighthouse or visiting an oyster farm.

The SoundWaters education staff includes environmental educators, crew and a master-licensed captain. College graduates with expertise in ecology, marine sciences or sailing are encouraged to apply for seasonal employment.

Program type Marine biology, English, environmental studies, special education, and full curriculum academics for middle, high-school and college students and adults.

Specs Sparred length: 80'. LOA: 64'10". LOD: 61'3". LWL: 58'10". Draft: 2'9" (min.); 8'8" (max.). Beam: 16'. Rig height: 60'. Freeboard: 3'6". Sail area: 1,510 sq. ft. Tons: 32 grt. Hull: steel. Designer: William Ward. Built: 1986; Marine Metals, Norfolk, Va. **Coast Guard cert.** Passenger vessel (Subchapter T). **Crew** 3; 5 instructors. Trainees: 42 (day). Age: 8+. Sex: co-ed. Dockside visitors: 52.

Contact Ruthann Shapiro, Executive Director, SoundWaters, Inc., Brewers Yacht Haven Marine Center, Washington Blvd., Stamford, CT 06902; 203 323-1978; FAX 203 967-8306.

SPIRIT OF MASSACHUSETTS

Rig topsail schooner, 2-masted. **Homeport/waters** Boston, Mass.: Atlantic Ocean and Caribbean.

Who sails? Student and other groups and individuals. Affiliated institutions include area schools; Long Island University. **Season** year round. **Cost** $92 per person per day. $2,000 per day for multi-day voyage with 22 trainees. $2,500 per day sail for 50.

Spirit of Massachusetts is modeled after the fishing schooner *Fredonia*, which was designed by Edward Burgess in 1889 and was popular for its beautiful appearance and speed. The design is typical of the Gloucester fishing schooners of the late 19th and early 20th centuries, the "fast and able" vessels which plied the rich Grand Banks and Georges Bank. The New England Historic Seaport's sail training schooner *Spirit of Massachusetts* was launched in 1984, and while traditional in design and construction, she conforms to all current U.S. Coast Guard safety requirements.

Aboard *Spirit of Massachusetts*, students participate in the operation of a traditional vessel and learn many skills including basic seamanship and navigation, with an introduction to the ocean's resources. Each program also has a unique historical, marine science or environmental theme. The skills acquired in sea experience under sail are personal ones: leadership, self-reliance, confidence and flexibility to successfully meet a variety of challenges both afloat and ashore.

Program type Sea education in marine science, maritime history and ecology in cooperation with accredited schools and colleges and other groups such as scouts.

Specs Sparred length: 125'. LOA: 103'. LOD: 100'. LWL: 80'. Draft: 10'6". Beam: 24'. Rig height: 103'. Freeboard: 7'. Sail area: 7,000 sq. ft. Tons: 90 grt. Power: 235 hp diesel. Hull: wood. Designer: Melbourne Smith and Andrew Davis. Built: 1984; New England Historic Seaport, Boston, Mass. **Coast Guard cert.** Sailing school vessel (Subchapter R). Passenger vessel (Subchapter T). **Crew** 7; 2 instructors. Trainees: 50 (day); 22 (overnight). Age: 15+. Sex: co-ed. Dockside visitors: 62.

Contact John Henderson, New England Historic Seaport, 197 Eighth Street, Charlestown Navy Yard, Boston, Mass. 02129; 617 242-1414; FAX 617 242-4322.

STAR OF INDIA

Former name *Euterpe.* **Rig** bark, 3-masted. **Homeport/waters** San Diego, Calif.: coastal waters between San Diego, Calif., and northern Baja California, Mexico.

Who sails? Affiliated institutions include San Diego, Orange County and Los Angeles public schools.

The oldest active square-rigger in the world, *Star of India* has been around the globe 21 times and never had an engine. Built as the full-rigged ship *Euterpe*, this former merchantman has survived countless perils of the sea to survive as a fully restored square rigger and National Historic Landmark. She embodies the term "tall ship" both in looks and spirit.

Star of India is the flagship of the San Diego Maritime Museum fleet. She sails infrequently but there are plans for an annual sailing schedule by 1997. *Star* is host to thousands of school children each year, many of whom participate in overnight living history programs on board. *Star*'s decks are also used for highly acclaimed cultural events from theatrical performances of *Two Years Before the Mast* and sea chantey festivals, to Gilbert & Sullivan comic operas and "Movies Before the Mast." Volunteer sail handling is held every other Sunday, with the best sailors being selected to sail the tall ship when she goes to sea.

Program type Sail training for crew and apprentices. Sea education in maritime history based on informal in-house programming. Dockside interpretation.

Specs Sparred length: 278'. LOD: 210'. LWL: 20'. Draft: 21'6". Beam: 35'. Rig height: 140'. Freeboard: 15'. Sail area: 18,000 sq. ft. Tons: 1,197 grt. Power: none. Hull: iron. Designer: Edward Arnold. Built: 1863; Gibson, McDonald & Arnold, Ramsey, Isle of Man. **Coast Guard cert.** Attraction vessel. Trainees: 140. Dockside visitors: 300.

Contact Joseph Ditler, Development Director, San Diego Maritime Museum, 1307 North Harbor Dr., San Diego, CA 92101; 619 234-9153; FAX 619 234-8345.

SUSAN CONSTANT

Rig bark, three-masted (lateen mizzen). **Homeport/waters** Jamestown, Va.: Chesapeake Bay.

Who sails? School groups from elementary school through college, individuals and families.

"On Saturday, the twentieth of December in the yeere 1606, the fleet fell from London," wrote George Percy, who kept an account of the voyage to Virginia. Three small ships — *Susan Constant* of 120 tons, *Godspeed* of 40 tons and *Discovery* of 20 tons — were underway on a voyage of colonization to the new world. On May 13, 1607 the colonists landed on Jamestown Island, named in honor of their king, England's first tiny foothold in the New World and that nation's first successful colony in North America

Today at Jamestown Settlement, a living history museum which recreates America's first permanent English settlement, the three ships have been accurately re-created and serve as working exhibits. To further the educational mission of the museum, a volunteer sail training program is offered to individuals of all ages. *Susan Constant* and *Godspeed* embark on several sail training and educational outreach voyages each year. Participants are trained in sailing a 17th-century merchant vessel including handling square sails, marlinespike seamanship, navigation, safety procedures, watch standing and maritime history.

Program type Sail training for crew and apprentices. Dockside interpretation.

Specs Sparred length: 116'. LOA: 96'. LOD: 83'. LWL: 77'. Draft: 11'6". Beam: 24'10". Rig height: 95'. Freeboard: 11'. Sail area: 3,902 sq. ft. Tons: 180 grt. Power: twin diesel. Hull: wood. Designer: Stanley Potter. Built: 1991; Allen C. Rawl, Jamestown, Va. **Crew** 25.

Contact Eric Speth, Maritime Program Manager, Jamestown Settlement, PO Drawer JF, Williamsburg, VA 23187; 804 229-1607; FAX 804 253-7350.

SWIFT OF IPSWICH

Rig square topsail schooner, 2-masted. **Homeport/waters** Los Angeles, Calif.: coastal California and offshore islands.

Who sails? Referred youth-at-risk and groups catering to students and adults. **Season** year round.

The Los Angeles Maritime Institute (LAMI), the educational affiliate of the Los Angeles Maritime Museum, operates the square topsail schooner *Swift of Ipswich*. LAMI staff use the ship to teach trainees how to sail and how to develop personal and "human skills" such as communication, cooperation, teamwork, persistence, self-reliance and leadership in three different programs.

Topsail is the basic outreach program, with participants recommended by people who work with youth, including educators, youth leaders and clergy. Cost is on an ability-to-pay basis. The program begins with a five-day series of day-sails followed by a five-day voyage planned and organized by the participants. Participants are encouraged to continue as active members of the "Swift Family."

Swift Expeditions are more advanced and challenging voyages with specific purposes, goals and durations. Cooperative programs afford organizations such as youth, church, school and community groups to voyage on *Swift of Ipswich*. The Los Angeles Maritime Museum and its affiliates take pleasure in offering assistance to visiting tall ships and other "educationally significant" vessels.

Program type Educational sailing adventures for "at-risk" youth and other youth or adult groups.

Specs Sparred length: 90'. LOA: 70'. LOD: 66'. LWL: 62'. Draft: 10'. Beam: 18'. Rig height: 74'. Freeboard: 5'. Sail area: 5,166 sq. ft. Tons: 46 grt. Power: diesel. Hull: wood. Designer: Howard I. Chapelle. Built: 1938; William A. Robinson, Ipswich, Mass. **Coast Guard cert.** Passenger vessel (Subchapter T). **Crew** 6. Trainees: 49 (day); 31 (overnight). Age: 12+. Sex: co-ed and unisex.

Contact James L. Gladson, Los Angeles Maritime Institute, Berth 84, Foot of Sixth St., San Pedro, CA 90731; 310 548-2902; FAX 310 832-6537.

SYLVINA W. BEAL

Rig gaff schooner, two-masted. **Homeport/waters** Mystic, Conn.: Lubeck, Me., to Sandy Hook, N.J.

Who sails? Indivdiuals, families and groups. Affiliated institutions include University of Massachusetts (Boston). **Season** April to November. **Cost** $750-$1,300 per day for 18 people, depending on the time of year, duration and program.

The *Sylvina W. Beal* has been in continuous operation since she was launched in 1911. A knockabout schooner, she was built for Charles Henry Beal who named her after his wife. The *Sylvina W. Beal* has always earned her keep. Initially, she was built as a mackerel seiner, then used in the herring fishery, buying the catch still held by the fishermen's nets and carrying it to canneries along the Maine coast. She also transported cargoes of haddock from Rockland to Gloucester, with barrels of molasses back to Rockland, and moved crated lobsters from Halifax. Occasionally, she hauled lumber, and in the days when it was still legal, she fished with dynamite.

In 1981, the *Sylvina W. Beal* was fitted out as a windjammer. She was structurally restored and equipped with the necessary safety gear to meet or exceed all U.S. Coast Guard requirements for passenger vessels. In her new role, she sailed for eight years along the coast of Maine. Captain Geoffrey Jones bought her in 1989 and now sails her in his home waters.

Program type Marine biology, maritime history, English and environmental studies for high school and college students.

Specs Sparred length: 84'. LOA: 80'. LWL: 70'. Draft: 8'. Beam: 17'. Rig height: 56'. Freeboard: 4'. Sail area: 2,200 sq. ft. Tons: 46 grt. Hull: wood. Built: 1911; East Boothbay, Maine. Builder: Frank J. Adams Yard; East Boothbay, Maine. **Coast Guard cert.** Passenger vessel (Subchapter T). **Crew** 4. Trainees: 30 (day);18 (overnight). Age: 14+. Sex: co-ed.

Contact Captain Geoffrey Jones, Sylvina W. Beal Cruises, Box 265, West Mystic, CT 06388; 203 536-8422.

TABOR BOY

Rig Dutch pilot schooner, 2-masted. **Homeport/waters** Marion, Mass.: coastal New England (summer); offshore Atlantic Ocean (school year).

Who sails? Enrolled students at Tabor Academy. **Cost** Included with regular tuition.

Tabor Boy has been engaged in sail training as a seagoing classroom for Tabor Academy students since 1954. Offshore voyaging and oceanographic studies go together in the curriculum, with cruises to destinations as distant as Mexico and Panama adding adventure to the experience. Many Tabor Academy graduates go on to the U.S. Merchant Marine, Navy or Coast Guard academies.

The schooner also offers seven summer orientation voyages for newly-enrolled freshmen and sophomore students. During this time, trainees are fully involved in sail handling, ship operation, navigation and seamanship. Harbor festivals and port visits along the New England coast are highlights of time spent ashore.

Program type Seamanship and oceanography for high school students.

Specs LOA: 92'. LWL: 82'6". Draft: 10'6". Beam: 21'9". Rig height: 95'. Sail area: 6,800 sq. ft. Tons: 99.9 grt. Power: 330 hp diesel. Built: 1914; Scheepswerven & Maschinenfabrik, Amsterdam, The Netherlands. **Coast Guard cert.** Sailing school vessel (Subchapter R). **Age:** 14-18. Sex: co-ed.

Contact Captain James Geil, Tabor Academy, Marion, MA 02738; 508 748-2000; FAX 508 748-0552.

Tecumseth, HMS

Rig topsail schooner, 2-masted. **Homeport/waters** Penetanguishene, Ontario: Georgian Bay, Lake Huron.

Who sails? Individuals and school groups. **Season** June-September. **Cost** Can $20 per person per two-hour sail.

Tecumseth is a replica of the 19th-century war schooner *Tecumseth* which served with the Royal Naval Establishment at Penetanguishene. Used for defense and transport duties from the Royal Navy base, she was an important component of the naval forces on the Upper Lakes. As on her sister-ship, the *Bee*, living history takes place aboard *Tecumseth*. New shipmates are sworn into the Royal Navy, trained and shipped out aboard a Royal Navy ship.

Although *Tecumseth* is a modern ship with up-to-date safety features, she is the mirror of her 1815 namesake and takes visitors back to the days of Nelson and England's "wooden walls." Once aboard, participants become one of the crew and make the ship come alive. Programs are open to anyone aged 10 and older. The *Tecumseth* takes a maximum of 45 trainees per sail. No previous experience is necessary.

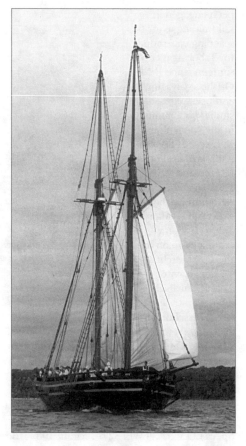

Program type Sail training for crew and apprentices.

Specs Sparred length: 125'. LOA: 80'. LOD: 70'. LWL: 63'. Draft: 8'. Beam: 29'. Rig height: 90'. Sail area: 4,700 sq. ft. Tons: 146 grt. Power: 360 hp diesel. Hull: steel. Designer: Bob Johnston. Built: 1994; Kanter Yachts, St. Thomas, Ontario. **Crew** 12. Trainees 45 (day). Age: 16+. Sex: co-ed.

Contact Chris Bagley, Coordinator, Discovery Harbour/Havre de la Découverte, Compartment 3, Box #12, 93 Jury Dr., Penetanguishene, Ontario L9M 1G1 Canada; 705 549-8064; FAX 705 549-4858.

TOLE MOUR

Rig square topsail schooner, 3-masted. **Homeport/waters** Honolulu, Hawaii: South Pacific.

Who sails? Trainees include emotionally impaired youth referred by the Hawaiian Department of Health, Child and Adolescent Mental Health Division. **Season** year round.

Built in 1988 to support primary health care and educational programs in Micronesia, *Tole Mour* ("gift of life and health") was named by the school children of the Marshall Islands. From 1988 through 1992, *Tole Mour* made regular teaching and medical "rounds" through the remote atolls of the Marshalls, serving 15,000 men, women and children in 58 far-flung communities. She carried multi-national teams of educators and health care professionals, most of whom served as volunteers. By the end of 1992, the volunteer professionals and health teams had been replaced entirely by Marshallese counterparts using powered patrol craft, which allowed Marimed to phase out support and bring *Tole Mour* home.

Since 1992, *Tole Mour* has been used to support programs for special needs adolescents, including youth referred by juvenile courts and adolescent mental health agencies. The ship currently supports a 6- to 12-month residential treatment program for Hawaiian youth who live, work and attend school on board while receiving group, individual and family therapy from a multidisciplinary treatment team.

Program type Vocational sail training leading to AB sail. Sea education in accredited high school and special education courses. Passenger day sails. Dockside interpretation during port visits.

Specs Sparred length: 156'. LOD: 123'. LWL: 101'. Draft: 13'6". Beam: 31'. Rig height: 110'. Freeboard: 6'. Sail area: 8,500 sq. ft. Tons: 229 grt. Power: 575 hp diesel. Hull: steel. Designer: Ewbank, Brooke & Assoc. Built: 1988; Nichols Bros., Seattle, Wash. **Coast Guard cert.** Sailing school vessel (Subchapter R); freight and miscellaneous (Subchapter I). **Crew** 11; 10 instructors. Trainees: 80 (day); 28 (overnight). Age: 13-25. Dockside visitors: 125.

Contact David D. Higgins, Marimed Foundation, 315 Uluniu Street, Suite 207, Kailua, Hawaii 96734; 808 261-8851; FAX 808 261-8246.

VICTORY CHIMES

Former name *Edwin and Maud.* **Rig** gaff schooner, 3-masted. **Homeport/waters** Rockland, Me.: coastal Maine.

Who sails? High school and college groups as well as individuals and adults of all ages. Affiliated institutions include Baylor Academy. **Season** June through September. **Cost** $100 per person per day.

Built in Bethel, Delaware, in 1900 the three-masted schooner *Victory Chimes* is the largest commercial sailing vessel under the American flag and the only original three-master still working in America. Recently nominated for National Historic Landmark status, the *Victory Chimes* has been quietly supporting herself and a succession of private owners for the past 95 years. She has never been part of a foundation nor

has she ever received any grants or endowments. She has been and continues to be a well maintained working vessel. Her current caretakers/owners Captain Kip Files and Captain Paul DeGaeta, offer Windjammer style vacations on Penobscot Bay. At over 200 gross tons, the *Victory Chimes* attracts career-minded professional crew and carries a crew of nine.

Program type Sail training for crew and apprentices and paying trainees. Sea education in marine science, maritime history and ecology based on informal in-house programming. Paying passengers on overnight passages.

Specs Sparred length: 170'. LOA: 140'. LOD: 132'. LWL: 127'. Draft: 7'5" (min.). Beam: 25'. Rig height: 87'. Freeboard: 11'. Sail area: 7,100 sq. ft. Tons: 208 grt. Power: yawl boat with 135 hp engine. Hull: wood. Designer: J. M. C. Moore. Built: 1900; Phillips & Co., Bethel, Del. **Coast Guard cert.** Passenger vessel (Subchapter T). **Crew** 10. Trainees: 44. Age: 16-75. Sex: co-ed.

Contact Captain Kip Files, Victory Chimes, Inc., PO Box 1401, Rockland, ME 04841; 207 594-0755.

Virginia

Rig Marconi sloop. **Homeport/waters** Dana Point, Calif.: coastal southern California.

Who sails? Individuals. **Season** year round. **Cost** $105 per student for 12-hour introduction to sailing; $155, 18-hour traditional sailing; and $255 for 30-hour advanced sailing.

Built in 1913, *Virginia* is a Q-Class sloop designed to race under the Universal Rule developed by Nathaniel Herreshoff in 1901. Indeed, the Q-Class boats were so fast that they were required to sail as a separate class within the Universal Rule. One of the few yachts named to the National Register of Historic Places (in 1991), *Virginia* has been sailed throughout her long career and is a three-time winner of the Chicago-Mackinac Race, winner of the Milwaukee, South Shore Yacht Club "Virginia Series" — which takes its name from the boat — and more than 30 smaller cups. *Virginia* is still sailed and raced in Southern California. In 1990, *Virginia* won first place and first to finish in the Bermuda Race, and in 1992, *Virginia* was first in class and first overall in the Long Beach-Dana Point race, and won the Dana Point series.

Virginia's sail training program focuses on helmsmanship, sail trim and yacht racing, and participants also practice all the crew positions for rigging, setting, jibing and dousing a spin-naker.

Program type Beginning through advanced sailing and ocean racing.

Specs Sparred length: 43'10". LOA: 43'10". LOD: 44'. LWL: 27'6". Draft: 6'. Beam: 8'6". Rig height: 56'. Freeboard: 2'. Sail area: 851 sq. ft. Sail no.: 47793. Tons: 14 grt. Hull: wood. Designer: William Gardner. Built: 1913; Wood & McClure Shipyard, City Island, N.Y. **Coast Guard cert.** Sailing school vessel (Subchapter R) and uninspected yacht. **Crew** 6-8; 1-2 instructors. Trainees: 6 (day). Age: adults. Sex: co-ed.

Contact Steve Christman, President, Nautical Heritage Society, 24532 Del Prado, Dana Point, CA 92629; 714 661-1001; FAX 714 240-7842.

WELCOME

Rig topsail sloop. **Homeport/waters** Traverse City, MI: Northern Great Lakes.

Who sails? Members of the Maritime Heritage Alliance. *Welcome* is affiliated with The Association for Great Lakes History.

The square topsail sloop *Welcome* is currently undergoing complete restoration at the Great Lakes Maritime Academy in Traverse City, Michigan by volunteer builders from the Maritime Heritage Alliance. The *Welcome* replicates faithfully the original sloop design. Built in 1775 at Mackinaw City, Michigan she was designed and served as a cargo hauler. She later was sold to the British military, armed with cannon and marines and guarded the strategically vital Straits of Mackinaw until her loss in 1781.

The restoration welcomes visitors to see traditional shipbuilding techniques applied to this lovely vessel. After completion *Welcome* will again sail and visit ports throughout the Great Lakes crewed by Maritime Heritage Alliance members.

Program Type Sail training and maritime history for students of all ages.

Specs Sparred length: 90'. LOA: 56'. LWL: 49'. Draft: 8'. Beam: 16'. Rig height: 96'. Freeboard: 6'. Tons: 45 grt. Power: Volvo diesel. Hull: wood. Designer: Fred Ford. Built: Ted McCutcheon; Mackinaw City, MI. **Coast Guard cert.** Attraction vessel. **Crew** 5. Trainees: 11. Age: 13+. Sex: co-ed.

Contact Linda Strauss, Director of Operations, Maritime Heritage Alliance, PO Box 1108, Traverse City, MI 49685-1108; 616 946-2647.

WESTWARD AND CORWITH CRAMER

Homeport/waters Woods Hole, Mass.: world wide.

Who sails? Affiliated institutions include Boston Univ., Colgate Univ., College of Charleston, Cornell Univ., Drexel Univ., Eckerd College, Franklin & Marshall College, Rice Univ., Univ. of Massachusetts and Univ. of Pennsylvania. In addition, more than 150 colleges and universities award full credit for SEA Semester. **Season** year round.

SEA Semesters on the research vessel *Westward* and *Corwith Cramer* (named for SEA's founder) offer college students a most complete undergraduate marine education experience. Combining studies ashore and at sea in marine sciences, maritime affairs and nautical science, *Westward*'s seagoing classroom attracts prominent scientists and educators, and college students compete for admission to this special program. Aboard ship, the twenty-four students stand eight hours of watch and attend two hours of lectures each day.

Their research projects are designed ashore to be carried out aboard this special sea-going laboratory. Students earn a full semester's academic credit (seventeen semester hours) for their participation.

Students spend the first half of a SEA Semester in Woods Hole receiving classroom and laboratory instruction in three ocean-related courses:

    • Introduction to oceanography (three credits), is a conceptual introduction to oceanography developed from its basis in biology, physics, chemistry and geology. The course provides a broad background in oceanography. Independent study projects developed ashore are carried out during the Sea Component.

• Introduction to maritime studies (three credits) is a multi-disciplinary study of the history, literature and art of our maritime heritage, and the political and economic problems of contemporary maritime affairs.

• Introduction to nautical science (three credits) is an introduction to the technologies (piloting, celestial and electronic), naval architecture, ship construction, marine engineering systems and the physics of sail taught from their basis in astronomy, mathematics and physics.

Students spend the second half of the SEA Semester aboard the research vessel *Westward*, enrolled in practical oceanography I (four credits) and practical oceanography II (four credits). Theories and problems raised in the shore component are tested in the practice of oceanography at sea aboard this modern 125' staysail schooner equipped for oceanographic data collection and staffed by scientists and professional officers. Students are instructed in the operation of basic oceanographic equipment, in the methodologies involved in the collection, reduction and analysis of oceanographic data, and in the attendant operations of a sailing oceanographic research vessel.

Program type Marine science, maritime history and literature.

Westward

Rig staysail schooner, 2-masted.

specs LOA: 125'. LWL: 84'. Draft: 13'. Beam: 22'. Sail area: 7,000 sq. ft. Tons: 138 grt. Power: 350 hp diesel. Hull: steel. Built: 1960-61; Abeking & Rasmussen, Lemwerder, Germany. Designer: Eldridge McInnis. **Coast Guard cert.** Sailing school vessel (Subchapter R). **Crew** 6; 4 instructors. Trainees: 24. Age: primarily college-age students, with some high school and postgraduate students. Sex: co-ed.

Corwith Cramer

Rig brigantine.

specs Sparred length: 134'. LOD: 98'. Draft: 13'. Beam: 26'. Rig height: 110'. Tons: 158 grt. Power: 500 hp diesel. Hull: steel. Built: 1987; ASTACE, Bilbao, Spain. **Coast Guard cert.** Sailing School Vessel (Subchapter R). **Crew** 6; 4 instructors. Trainees: 24. Age: Primarily college-age students, with some high school and postgraduate students. Sex: co-ed.

Contact Sea Education Association (SEA) Inc., PO Box 6, Woods Hole, MA 02543; 508 540-3954; 800 552-3633; FAX 508 457-4673.

WILLIAM H. ALBURY

Former names *Heritage of Miami, William H. Albury.* **Rig** gaff topsail schooner, 2-masted.
Homeport/waters Miami, Fla.: Biscayne Bay, Florida Keys, and Bahamas.

Who sails? School and other groups and individuals. Affiliated institutions include Boy
Scouts, Dade County, Broward County and Abaco, Bahamas, schools. **Cost** $75 per person
per day; $600 group rate.

In an era when the Atlantic crossing is measured in hours rather than weeks and most people's occupations anchor them to a desk, counter or workbench, Sea Exploring offers a learning-by-doing environment whose lessons of character and cooperation apply to all facets of one's life. The Sea Explorer program requires that each trainee exert and extend him or herself physically, morally and mentally in order to perform his or her duties and to contribute to the teamwork needed of shipmates. The reward, over and above the experience of a world of beauty and challenge, is the satisfaction and self-assurance that contributes to self-discipline. The *William H. Albury*'s Sea Explorer program offers lessons in ecology and international cooperation, as well as history, science, literature and art. Subject constantly to the dictates of nature, the Sea Explorer program is fun, adventuresome and a wonderful developer of character and molder of lives.

Program type Sail training with crew and apprentices and paying trainees. Sea education in
maritime history and ecology in cooperation with accredited schools and colleges and other
groups. Passenger day sail and overnight passages.

Specs Sparred length: 70'. LOA: 60'. LOD: 56'. LWL: 49'. Draft: 6'. Beam: 14'. Rig
height: 64'. Freeboard: 6'. Sail area: 2,100 sq. ft. Tons: 24 grt. Power: 150 hp GM-453 diesel.
Hull: wood. Designer: traditional, Bahamas Banks schooner. Built: 1964; William H. Albury,
Man o' War Cay, Abaco, Bahamas. **Coast Guard cert.** Sailing school vessel (Subchapter R).
Passenger vessel (Subchapter T). **Crew** 3. Trainees: 30 (day); 14 (overnight). Dockside visitors: 30.

Contact Captain Joseph A. Maggio, Marine Superintendent, Inter-Island Schooner, 3145
Virginia St., Coconut Grove, FL 33133; 305 442-9697; FAX 305-442-9697.

WILLIAM H. THORNDIKE

Rig gaff schooner. **Homeport/waters** New Hampshire: unlimited.

Who sails? High school through college age students, adults, and families. **Season** year round.

The schooner *William H. Thorndike*, corporate flagship of the Meridith, NH - based Annalee Mobilitee Dolls, Inc. is based in New England after a 20-year absence. While docked in San Francisco in the summer of 1993, the boat sailed in the 1st annual Parade of Tall Ships on the west coast. The *William H. Thorndike* is the recepient of numerous awards over the years — the most significant being the recent trophy for sportsmanship "over and above the call of duty" at the 7th annual Camden Wooden Yacht Regatta. Committed to seamanship, the captain and crew of the *William H. Thorndike* enjoy competing in the many regattas that occur throughout the year.

A longtime member the Master Mariners Association, a group made up of traditional vessels that fosters comaraderie through the social gatherings of the ships and light-hearted competition; all on board the *William H. Thorndike* invite those interested in seamanship and sail training to contact them to find out more about sail training opportunities on board the *William H. Thorndike*.

Program Type Sail training and seamanship for trainees of all ages.

Specs Sparred length: 75'. LOA: 65'. LOD: 65'. LWL: 50'. Draft: 8'6". Beam: 15'. Rig height: 60'. Tons: 43 grt. Power: Diesel. Hull: wood. Designer: Sam Crocker. Built: 1939; Sims Brothers, doc. #239013 **Crew** 4. Trainees: 6

Contact Townsend Thorndike, 50 Reservoir Road, PO Box 708, Meredith, NH 03253-0708; 603 279-3333.

WINDY

Rig gaff topsail schooner, 4-masted. **Homeport/waters** Chicago, Ill.: Great Lakes, East Coast and Caribbean.

Who sails? Affiliated institutions include the Chicago Navy Pier. **Season** June-September, Chicago; October-May, East Coast. **Cost** $10-$100 per person, depending on cruise.

Windy, the tall ship of Chicago, the windy city, operates out of the newly-renovated Navy Pier during the summer months. During the fall, winter and spring, *Windy* will embark on a cruise south via the Great Lakes and Erie Canal to the east coast of the United States and the Caribbean. Completed in 1996, she is the first four-masted schooner built in the United States since 1921. She is a unique blend of the best traditions and modern materials and safety features. She has many features not found in other vessels, including 10 private cabins, a bunk room for 12, library, bow thruster, shoal draft and wing keel.

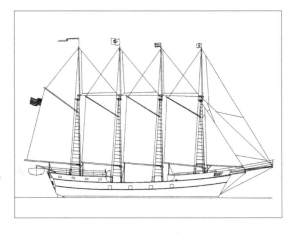

Windy's sail training programs focusing on maritime heritage and nautical science are individually designed for groups of up to 150 for day cruises and 26 overnight. Programs are adapted to scouts, seniors, church groups, schools, corporations and others. Full participation in all functions of the vessel are encouraged. *Windy* is ideal for private charters, including corporate functions, team building activities, receptions, weddings and other private celebrations.

Program type Maritime Heritage and Nautical Science education programs, public recreation cruises and private charters.

Specs Sparred length: 148'. LOA: 109'. LOD: 109'. LWL: 93'. Draft: 8'. Beam: 25'. Rig height: 85'. Freeboard: 7'. Sail area: 5,000 sq. ft. Tons: 140 disp. Power: 300 hp Cummins. Hull: steel. Designer: R. Marthai. Built: 1996; Detyens Shipyard/Southern Windjammer, Ltd. **Coast Guard cert.** Passenger vessel (Subchapter T). **Crew**: instructors. Trainees: 150 (day); 26 (overnight). Sex: co-ed.

Contact Captain Robert Marthai, Windy of Chicago, Ltd. Summer: 600 East Grand Ave., Chicago, IL 60611; 312 595-5555. Other seasons: 2044 Wappoo Hall Rd., Charleston, SC 29412; 803 762-1342.

YANKEE

Rig gaff topsail schooner. **Homeport/waters** Cape May, N.J.: Atlantic Ocean from Sandy Hook, N.J., to Key West, Fla.

Who sails? Middle and high school groups as well as individuals and families of all ages.

The gaff topsail schooner *Yankee* was the last vessel built in historic Gardiners Basin in Atlantic City, New Jersey. Since her launch in 1982, she has sailed the length of the U.S. east coast from Eastport, Maine, to Key West, Florida, doing three-hour day sails and overnight cruises.

Yankee was purchased by Sail America, Inc. in 1986 and is presently operated by Captain Dave Franchetta and his wife Peggy. During the summer she sails out of Cape May, New Jersey, and in the winter from Key Largo, Florida. Fall months are reserved for three- and four-day cruises on the Chesapeake Bay. Both captain and crew welcome you aboard *Yankee* for a "Tall Ship Adventure."

Program type Sail training for crew, apprentices and paying trainees. Sea education in maritime history and ecology based on informal in-house programming. Passenger day sails and overnight passengers.

Specs Sparred length: 78'. LOA: 65'. LOD: 64'. LWL: 50'. Draft: 6'6". Beam: 17'. Rig height: 64'. Freeboard: 5'. Sail area: 2,400 sq. ft. Tons: 50 grt. Power: 120 hp. Hull: steel. Designer: Merritt Walter. Built: 1982; Dan Hallock, Atlantic City, N.J. **Coast Guard cert**. Passenger vessel (Subchapter T). **Crew** 3. Trainees: 46.

Contact Peggy Franchetta, Activities Coordinator, Sail America, Inc., PO Box 98, Cape May, NJ 08204; 609 884-1919; FAX 609 886-9003.

ZODIAC

Rig schooner. **Homeport/waters** Seattle, WA: Puget Sound, San Juan Islands, Canadian Gulf Islands.

Who sails? High school through college age students, adults, and families. **Season** year round. **Cost** $100 per person per day. Group rate $2,000 group rate per day.

The circumstances of *Zodiac's* design, construction, and livelihood are woven like thread through the fabric of the twentieth century. As *Zodiac*, she was designed to reflect the highest achievement of naval architecture under working sail. Yet, she was fundamentally a yacht. Built in 1924 for the Johnson & Johnson Pharmaceutical Company, she raced the Atlantic from Sandy Hook, New Jersey to Spain in 1928. The crash of 1929 forced her sale to the San Francisco Pilots Association in 1931.

Renamed *California*, she began a proud 40 years off the Golden Gate. She was the largest schooner ever operated by the Bar Pilots, and worked in that capacity until 1972. She was purchased again in 1975 by a group of young craftsmen experienced in wooden boat restoration and was renamed *Zodiac*.

In 1982 she was place on the National Register of Historic Places, the official list of the nation's cultural treasures worthy of preservation, as a tangible reminder of the maritime history of the United States. Certified by the Coast Guard as a passenger vessel, she operates Puget Sound, the San Juan Islands, and the Canadian Gulf Coast. *Zodiac's* spaciousness and amenities make her the ideal boat for sail training and sea education that are popular with a wide range of people.

In early spring and late fall *Zodiac* conducts 13 Elderhostel sessions keeping the volunteer crew on their toes teaching sailing, navigation, Northwest Indian culture, legends of the Pig War Island, and geology and natural resources of the San Juan Islands. Summer sessions are open to sailing enthusiast sixteen years and older who want to learn to handle the great sails and stand watches on the helm and in the chart room.

Program Type Sail training for trainees of all ages, marine sciences, maritime history, environmental studies, and Elderhostel for adults.

Specs Sparred length: 160'. LOA: 127'. LOD: 127'. LWL: 101'. Draft: 16'. Beam: 26'. Rig height: 101'. Freeboard: 5'. Sail area: 7,000 sq. ft. Tons: 147 grt. Power: diesel. Hull: wood. Designer: William Hand, Jr. Built: 1924; Hodgdon Brothers; East Boothbay, ME. **Coast Guard cert.** Passenger vessel (Subchapter T). **Crew** 8. Trainees: 49

Contact June Mehrer, President, Vessel Zodiac Corporation, PO Box 322, Snohomish, WA 98290; 206 483-4088; FAX 206 676-9778.

MORE ASTA MEMBERS

WORKS IN PROGRESS
OUTSIDE NORTH AMERICA
OTHER PROJECTS

Amistad Project WORK IN PROGRESS

Rig tops'l schooner. **Homeport/waters** New Haven, CT: East Coast.

Who sails? School groups from elementary school through college, individuals, and families. Court referrals for some groups. The *Amistad* Project is associated with Mystic Seaport.

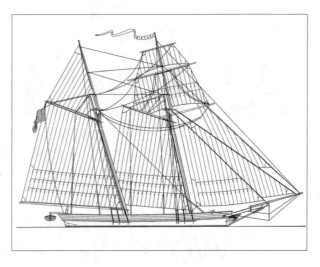

The *Amistad's* story began in June 1839 when a group of kidnapped Africans from what is now Sierra Leone, West Africa were sold illegally as slaves in Havana, Cuba. Led by Sengbe Pieh (Cinque) the captives took command of the merchant schooner *L'Amistad* and attempted to return to their homeland. After 63 days the vessel was seized off Montauk Point, Long Island by the brig *Washington*. A lengthy federal court battle ended when their case was successfully argued before the Supreme Court by former President John Quincy Adams. In 1841 the captured Africans were returned home.

The Connecticut Afro-American Historical Society, with the assistance of the State of Connecticut, Department of Economic and Community Development, is seeking to perpetuate the legacy of the freedom schooner *Amistad*. Designed and built as a working vessel, the reproduction, *Amistad*, will travel to ports throughout the country to serve as a floating classroom, museum, theater and youth center. Plans call for on-board exhibits, interpretation, and sail training programs. Construction is to take place at Mystic Seaport.

Program Type Sail training for crew/apprentices and with paying trainees. Maritime history, and a full range of programming is expected. Passenger day and overnight sails and dockside interpretation during home and port visits.

Specs Sparred length: n/a. LOA: n/a. LOD: n/a. LWL: n/a. Draft: n/a. Beam: n/a. Rig height: n/a. Freeboard: n/a. Sail area: n/a sq. ft. Tons: n/a. Power: diesel. Hull: wood. Designer: Tri-Coastal Marine. Built: current; Mystic Seaport Mystic, CT. **Coast Guard cert.** n/a. **Crew** n/a. Trainees: n/a.

Contact Khalid Lum, President, Connecticut Afro-American Historical Society, Dixwell Community House, 197 Dixwell Avenue, New Haven, CT 06511; 203 867-8737; FAX 203 867-8739.

Anawan WORK IN PROGRESS

Rig bugeye ketch. **Homeport/waters** Bar Harbor: Maine coast.

The *Anawan* is a replica of a bugeye, a working sail vessel developed in the 19th century on Chesapeake Bay and used primarily for oystering and freighting. Designed by Russell Grinnell, *Anawan* was built in the Crocker Boat Yard for his own use. She has been used both as a private vessel and as a sail-training vessel, and she has participated in at least two tall ship gatherings. The *Anawan* underwent restoration in 1995 and will be operating from Bar Harbor, Maine. Her handy bugeye rig and shallow draft will enable her to cruise the bays and shoreline near Acadia National Park. Her classic wooden hull and rakish traditional appearance will be maintained by supervised apprentice crew who will also learn basic seamanship while serving on board. The *Anawan* will also sail with up to six passengers on excursions and island hopping.

Program type Sail training for crew and apprentices. Passenger day sails. Dockside interpretation.

Specs Sparred length: 56'. LOD: 37'. Draft: 2'6". Beam: 12'9". Tons: 7 grt. Power: diesel. Hull: wood. Designer: Russell Grinnell. Built: 1960; Crocker Boat Yard, Manchester, Mass. **Crew** 2. Trainees: 6. Sex: co-ed.

Contact Captain Steven F. Pagels, Downeast Windjammer Cruises, PO Box 8, Cherryfield, ME 04622; 207 546-2927; FAX 207 546-2023.

Moshulu OTHER PROJECTS

Rig Bark, 4-masted. **Home-port/waters** Philadelphia, Pa.

One of the largest merchant sailing ships ever built, *Moshulu* was built for a German firm for work in the nitrate trade, sailing from Hamburg and around Cape Horn to ports in Chile. In 1917, she was acquired by California interests and spent the next 11 years in transpacific trade. After seven years laid up in Puget Sound, she was bought by the great merchant sailing ship owner Gustaf Erikson and entered the Australian grain trade under the Finnish flag. During World War II, she was laid up in Norway and used as a grain storage ship until 1970 when she was bought for use as a floating restaurant in Philadelphia.

Specs Sparred length: 394'. Draft: 12'. Beam: 48'. Rig height: 198'. Freeboard: 22'. Tons: 3,116 grt. Hull: iron. Built: 1904; William Hamilton & Co., Port Glasgow, Scotland.

Contact Eli Karetny, "HMS" Ventures, Pier 34, 735 South Columbus Blvd., Philadelphia, PA 19147; 215 923 2500; FAX 215 829-1604.

PICTON CASTLE WORK IN PROGRESS

Rig bark, 3-masted. **Homeport/waters** British Virgin Islands: deep-water voyages, round-the-world cruises.

Currently undergoing refit, the bark *Picton Castle* will be devoted to making long voyages with expense-sharing amateur crew under the direction of experienced professionals. The first voyage planned is an 18-month, round-the-world voyage, followed by shorter voyages to the South Pacific, the Canadian Maritimes, Europe, the West Indies, and around the world again. The vessel, to be rigged as a three-masted bark, was built in England in 1928 of riveted steel, employing the finest in old-world design and craftsmanship. She will be a safe and comfortable home afloat for a few fortunate adventurers under the experienced command of Captain Daniel Moreland. The mission of the *Picton Castle* is to take folks deep-sea as crew in a strong, well found square-rigged ship to learn the arts of the seafarer and see the world. The vessel also has a 200-ton cargo hold for trading goods and supplies between the remoter islands of the tropics.

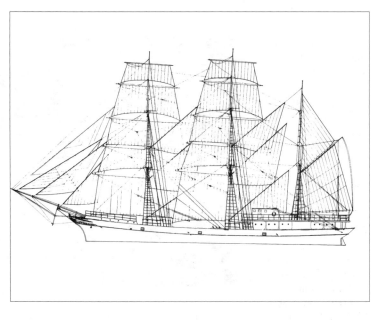

Program type Sail training with paying trainees.

Specs Sparred length: 178'. LOA: 152'. LOD: 139'. LWL: 130'. Draft: 14'. Beam: 24'. Rig height: 100'. Freeboard: 5'. Sail area: 12,500 sq. ft. Tons: 299 grt. Power: 690 hp diesel. Hull: steel. Built: 1928; Cochran's Ship Builder, Selby, England. **Crew** 11. Trainees: 35. Sex: co-ed.

Contact Captain Daniel Moreland, Windward Isles Sailing Ship Co. Ltd., Box 18, Rowayton, CT 06833; 203 838-7894, 203 866-0182.

Robertson Project WORK IN PROGRESS

Rig gaff topsail schooner, 2-masted. **Homeport/waters** Victoria, B.C.: Pacific Northwest, Pacific Ocean.

Who sails? Elementary through college age students. **Season** March to October. **Cost** Can $55 per day per trainee.

Since the retirement of SALTS' flagship, the *Robertson II*, at the end of the 1995 sail training season, a new *Robertson* has been taking shape at the SALTS' Heritage Shipyard in the inner harbor at Victoria, British Columbia. The lines of the old ship, one of Canada's last original Grand Banks fishing schooners, have been carefully taken off and a new replica vessel is well underway.

Construction is of double-sawn fir frames, and she is the largest wooden sailing vessel presently being built in Canada using traditional methods. The boat building team consists largely of skippers and crew members of other SALTS vessels, ably assisted by volunteers and past trainees.

The maiden voyage is scheduled to take place in the year 2000 with a 22-month world circumnavigation. The new *Robertson* will join the *Pacific Swift* in providing both coastal and offshore sail training voyages for approximately 1,000 young people each year.

Program type Maritime history and nautical instruction.

Specs Sparred length: 130'. LOA: 107'10". LOD: 105'. LWL: 93'. Draft: 11'. Beam: 22'2". Rig height: 105'. Freeboard: 5'. Sail area: 5,637 sq. ft. Tons: 170 grt. Power: twin diesels. Hull: wood. Designer: traditional Grand Banks schooner. Built: under construction; SALTS, Victoria, British Columbia. **Coast Guard cert.** Canadian passenger vessel and sailing school vessel. **Crew** 5; 3 instructors. Trainees: 40 (day); 30 (overnight).

Contact Captain Martyn J. Clark, Executive Director, Sail and Life Training Society (SALTS), PO Box 5014, Station B, Victoria, British Columbia V8R 6N3 Canada; 604 383-6811; FAX 604 383-7781.

Sovereign of the Seas OUTSIDE NORTH AMERICA

Rig barquentine. **Homeport/waters** Freemantle, Western Australia: Indian and Pacific Oceans.

Who sails? College students, adults, and families. Special Education program designed for the handicapped. Affiliated with Ashronia Ministries and Western Australia colleges. **Cost:** $50.00 per person per day.

The *Sovereign of the Seas*, owned and operated by Ashronia Ministries in Western Australia, will sail as a supply vessel with the proviso to assist and foster a greater understanding for the less fortunate of this world. Accomplishing this in practical ways, the vessel has been designed to accommodate a co-ed crew of all physical abilities and all age groups.

Sovereign of the Seas plans to sail with both able-bodied and physically handicapped cadets who will share the challenges in character building and leadership training a square-rigged ship offers. By design, equipped with two cargo holds for relief materials, food, clothing, medical supplies and a ten-bed hospital; the vessel provides a very special mercy aid to needy ports. During the summer months she will operate in local waters and then with the coming winter gales she will seek northern waters on international cruises.

Program Type A fully accredited sail training vessel for missionary cadets offering maritime history and navigational studies.

Specs Sparred length: 200'. LOA: 162'. LOD: 155'. LWL: 145'. Draft: 15'. Beam: 38'. Rig height: 118'. Freeboard: 12'. Sail area: 10,000 sq. ft. Tons: 130 grt. Power: Yanmar T220. Hull: steel. Designer: L. Shave. Built: 1998 (projected); Transfield, Western Australia. **Crew** 12. Trainees: 60 (day); 30 (overnight). Dockside visitors: 200. Sex: co-ed.

Contact Lawrence (Lofty) Shave, Pastor/Administrator, Ashronia Christian Cadet & Mission Ship Association, PO Box 1207, Fremantle, Western Australia, 6160; 09-335-2230; FAX 09-430-8040.

Young America WORK IN PROGRESS

Rig gaff topsail schooner, 2-masted.

Homeport/waters Bar Harbor, Me./Atlantic City, N.J.: East Coast between Maine and Chesapeake Bay.

Originally built in 1976 as a brigantine, the *Young America* is undergoing an intensive two-year rebuilding in Southwest Harbor, Maine. The *Young America* formerly operated as a sail training and passenger vessel out of Atlantic City, New Jersey. Purchased by Captain Pagels, the *Young America* will emerge from her rebuilding with a two-masted topsail rig. Upon commencing her sailing career again, the schooner *Young America* will participate in sail training activities, as well as chartering. She will divide her time between Bar Harbor, Maine, and Atlantic City, New Jersey. Cruises offered will be both day sails and overnight passages. Sail training cruises will stress vessel maintenance and responsibility along with sail handling and coastal navigation. The *Young America* (named for the famed clipper ship) is patterned after a 19th-century merchant vessel, and with her broad decks and high bulwarks she has the feel a large vessel.

Program type Passenger day sails and overnight passages. Dockside interpretation.

Specs Sparred length: 130'. LOA: 94'. LOD: 90'. Draft: 9'6". Beam: 24'. Rig height: 85'. Sail area: 3,400 sq. ft. Tons: 94 grt. Power: diesel. Hull: ferro-cement. Designer: Charles Wittholz. Built: 1976; David Kent, Port Jefferson, N.Y. **Coast Guard cert**. Passenger vessel (Subchapter T). **Crew** 4 (day); 6 (overnight). Trainees: 100 (day); 30 (overnight).

Contact Captain Steven F. Pagels, PO Box 8, Cherryfield, ME 04622; 207 546-2927; FAX 207 546-2023.

ASTA

SAIL TRAINING

PROGRAMS

ActionQuest/ActionSail Programs

ActionQuest Programs offers ActionSail for teens ages 13 to 19, an opportunity to learn sailing while living aboard a boat and cruising throughout the British Virgin and Leeward Islands. Shipmates sail in a fleet and rotate positions daily, acting as skipper, mate, navigator, cook, ship's husband, sail trimmer and bosun. Each sailor is fully involved in ship operation and seamanship while receiving certification training in diving, windsurfing, water skiing, celestial navigation and other maritime skills. Harbor visits and shore excursions while in port, and Motive Power programs offered in the evenings aboard, assist young adults to recognize, organize and accomplish their goals.

ActionQuest uses various sailing vessels in their program and operates during the summer months. Cost per session (three to six weeks) runs from $2,385 to $2,880. The programs use the British Virgin Islands and St. Maarten as home ports and sail the Virgin and Leeward Islands. Staff opportunities are also available. Licensed individuals interested in summer employment are encouraged to apply.

Captain James Stoll, ActionQuest Programs.

AndaVela

The AndaVela program seeks to train people in the art of sailing and to foster an appreciation for the uniqueness of the fragile marine ecosystem of Cape Verde. Cape Verde is an archipelago of 10 islands located off the coat of West Africa. A long tradition of boat building, fishing and transport of cargo and people by sail has been a part of the life and economy on those islands. This tradition is the primary impetus for the creation of the AndaVela program. Through cooperation and education, the program will build awareness of the importance of sailing, develop a shore school and on the water training courses, establish guidelines for peer training courses and encourage community involvement. A major emphasis of the training program will be to provide positive activities for young people who are now faced with the problems of rapid urban development in a country once dominated by rural and marine endeavors.

This is a start-up year for AndaVela. The directors are equipping the 25-foot sloop *Kokopelii* for coastal sailing. There are further plans to acquire and/or build a fleet of sail training boats. Cape Verde has few financial and educational resources, and the directors welcome input from abroad.

Cynthia Durost and Emmanuel Bettencourt, Co-Directors, AndaVela, 73-75 Rua Justino Lopes, Praia, Cape Verde; 011 238-61-30-21.

Artisans College

The Artisans College uses boat building and design as a way of developing manual skills in an academic setting. The College offers a two-year Associate of Science degree as well as one-year interim programs. The mission of the college is to nurture, educate and train builders, artists and artisans to think creatively, to work effectively, and to achieve in practice what they envision in their imagination.

Through its program of academic studies and manual skills, the College gives a student the math and analytical skills to design an object, the manual skills to build an object, and the business and communications skills to promote and market an object.

The program includes the building of high-tech racing yachts, experimental prototypes and historic reproductions. Academic courses — which include marine architecture, design, math, physics, English, business, philosophy and history courses — are woven into the course of study to provide a foundation in writing, business practice and the humanities. In addition to a two-year Associate of Science degree, the college also offers an optional third and fourth year, by invitation only, for students who have completed the two-year course of study.

Archie D. McRee, Director of Admissions, The Artisans College, Elm St., PO Box 539, Rockport, ME 04856; 207 236-6071; FAX 207 236-8367.

Atlantic Challenge

Atlantic Challenge was built on Kurt Hahn's cry to "impel youth into life-giving experiences", to "train through and for the sea", to connect those of many nations in the same boats, and to seek Athenian means of encouraging and training youth to compassionate service and community-building. Small, elegant boats and intricate rigs are chosen – these craft were drawn from the ingenuity of fisherman, who for centuries have built for safe sea-keeping and ease of repair. Technically considered longboats, or admiral barges, Atlantic Challenge has coined the terms "Bantries" or "Gigs".

Every two years a growing number of nations rendezvous in a different host country for a friendly ten-day Contest of Seamanship (not racing!). Seamanship is defined as, "What you do when you don't know what to do", as useful a skill on land as on sea, in the cities, or the plains. The crews are Ambassadors in Seaboots; they meet one another, parade their own skills, and partake of a feast of experiences - the sea, connections, and comradeship.

Lance R. Lee, President, Atlantic Challenge Foundation, PO Box B, Rockland, ME 04841; 207 594-1800; FAX 207 594-5056.

Bay Area
Convention and Visitors Bureau

The Bay Area Convention and Visitors Bureau of Bay City, Michigan, hosts various schooner and tall ship sailing adventures, open to the public, from spring through the fall.

These cruises leave from Bay City, on the Saginaw River, and venture into the Saginaw Bay. Special corporate cruises and bed and breakfast cruises are generally available.

Shirley Roberts, 901 Saginaw St., Bay City, MI 48705-5614; 517 893-1222; FAX 517 893-7016.

BOAT/U.S.
Foundation for Boating Safety

The BOAT/U.S. Foundation for Boating Safety is a non-profit boating safety education and research organization which operates a toll-free CourseLine for information on free boating courses at 800 336-2628. The foundation also researches boating accidents and safety issues, produces and distributes free safety literature, maintains a national recreational boating reference library, promotes boating education and tests safety products.

James F. Ellis, Executive Vice President, BOAT/US Foundation for Boating, 880 South Pickett St., Alexandria, VA 22304; 703 823-9550; FAX 703 461-2855.

Columbus Santa Maria, Inc.

The *Santa Maria* is a full-scale museum-quality representation of Christopher Columbus' flagship. She is berthed in the Scioto River in downtown Columbus, Ohio, the largest city in the world named for Christopher Columbus. The *Santa Maria* was built for the Columbus 1992 Quincentennial Celebration from Martinez Hidalgo's plans as adapted and provided by the Kingdom of Spain. While she is rigged to sail, she is primarily operated as a dockside exhibit and educational vessel due to space limitations of the Scioto River.

The *Santa Maria* is owned and operated by Columbus Santa Maria, an Ohio charitable not-for-profit organization. In addition to being open to the public for daily tours, a wide variety of educational programs are offered for youth and adults. Small boatbuilding and rowing programs complement the sail handling courses offered on the ship.

Tara Barney, Columbus Santa Maria, Inc., 50 West Gay Street, Columbus, OH 43215; 614 645-8760.

Dirigo Cruises

Captain Eben M. Whitcomb, Jr. 39 Waterside Lane, Clinton, CT 06413; 203 669-7068; FAX 203 669-2297.

East End Seaport Marine Foundation

The East End Seaport and Marine Foundation, a not-for-profit organization, was founded to preserve, restore and recognize the marine and seaport history of Eastern Long Island. Its programs and activities include the maintenance of Long Beach Bar "Bug" Lighthouse at the entrance to Peconic Bays. It also maintains the East End Seaport Maritime Museum, which features exhibits about sea life, aids to navigation, local shipbuilding history, yacht racing (including the America's Cup), and an original fourth-order Fresnel lens. In addition, the Foundation is restoring a century-old marine railway for the purpose of servicing historic tall ships, and it is one of two organizations supporting the restoration of the wooden barkentine, *Regina Maris*. Each fall the foundation sponsors the East End Seaport Maritime Festival, featuring whale boat races and a wooden boat regatta, and in October the Foundation hosts the annual scallop festival.

Merlon E. Wiggin, East End Seaport Marine Foundation One Bootleg Alley, PO Box 624, Greenport, NY 11944; 516 477-0004; 516 477-0198.

Hands On Sail Training, Inc.

Captain Dutch Shultis, 3 Church St., #234, Annapolis, MD 21401; 410 268-0647.

Independence Seaport Museum

The Independence Seaport Museum is located on the Delaware River at Penn's Landing in downtown Philadelphia. The Museum is a private, non-profit institution dedicated to the collection, preservation, and interpretation of materials relating to maritime history, with a particular emphasis on the Delaware Bay and River.

Located in a newly-renovated, multi-million dollar facility, the Museum houses permanent and changing exhibit galleries, classrooms, an active boatbuilding shop, and a specialized maritime library. Museum visitors can tour the 1944 U. S. Navy submarine *Becuna* and the cruiser *Olympia*, launched in 1895. The 1934 Trumpy motor yacht *Enticer* is maintained and operated in the charter trade.

The Museum regularly provides berths for visiting vessels and has jointly offered educational programs with sail training vessels such as, *Niagara, A. J. Meerwald, Pioneer,* and *Mimi*.

Paul DeOrsay, Assistant Director, Independence Seaport Museum, 211 South Columbus Boulevard, Philadelphia, PA 19106; 215 925-5439; FAX 215 925-6713.

Jamestown Marine Services

Bruce Banks, 24 Southwest Avenue, PO Box 629, Jamestown, RI 02835; 401 423-3144.

Kalmar Nyckel Shipyard

The Kalmar Nyckel Foundation has embarked on an enthusiastic project to build a working replica of the 1629 Dutch pinnace *Kalmar Nyckel*, which landed the first Swedes and Finns in North America in 1638. The Kalmar Nyckel Project is a complex of historical, cultural and educational facilities and programs. The *Kalmar Nyckel*, presently under construction and scheduled to be completed in the spring of 1997, will be used as a focal point for Wilmington waterfront revitalization.

Margaret Tigue Fillos, Executive Director, Kalmar Nyckel Foundation, 1124 East 7th St., Wilmington, DE 19801; 302 429-SHIP; FAX 302 429-0350.

Lorain (Ohio) Port Authority

Lorain, Ohio, is a working waterfront located at the mouth of the Black River on the southern shore of Lake Erie, midway between Cleveland and Sandusky. Phase I of the 1986 Strategic Development Plan for Lorain's harbor area, including marinas, retail and public open space, and recreational facilities, is complete.

Development of two new projects will begin in 1996. The 20-acre Black River Boat Ramp Project will provide a six-lane public launch site with commercial/retail shops and public open space. The 22-acre "Grove Site" Project will create a well-balanced mixed-use development. Proposed uses for the site include a Riverwalk, Transportation Center, Industrial Heritage Museum and Festival Grounds.

The Lorain Port Authority also sponsors the Port Awareness Weekend and Lighthouse Celebration, held annually the second weekend in June (June 6-9, 1996) to celebrate the development occurring along the waterfront. There is continuous live entertainment on three stages and activities for all ages, including artists' displays, waterfront exhibits and demonstrations, a boat show, car show and children's rides.

Joanette Romero, Lorain Port Authority, Room 511, City Hall, 200 West Erie Avenue, Lorain, OH 44052; 216 244-2269.

Metropolitan Pier and Exposition Authority

Just east of Chicago's downtown area on Lake Michigan, Navy Pier has been a Chicago landmark since 1916. With more than 50 acres of parks, exhibitions facilities, shops, restaurants and attractions, the New Navy Pier, which opened in the summer of 1995, offers unequaled views of the magnificent skyline and lakefront. Host to several sight-seeing boats and dinner cruise ships, the Pier will boast its own 145-foot four-masted schooner, *Windy*, beginning in May 1996. Docked across from RIVA Restaurant at the west end of the Festival hall, *Windy* will provide two-hour public cruises, private charters and educational cruises daily.

Jerome R. Butler, Senior Director of Development, Navy Pier, Metropolitan Pier and Exposition Authority, 600 East Grand Ave., Chicago, IL 60611; 312 595-5100, 800 595-PIER; FAX 312 791-6572.

New Jersey Seafood Festival

The New Jersey Fresh Seafood Festival, held annually on the second weekend in June, was organized in 1989 to raise money for local charities, promote ocean awareness and support the state's fishing and seafood industries. A tall ship is the featured attraction at each festival. Most recently, the *Lettie G. Howard*, provided tours to 18,000 festival goers who came out for the great food, crafts, exhibits and entertainment that make the New Jersey Fresh Seafood Festival in Atlantic City one of the hottest weekends at the Jersey shore.

Lauralee Dobbins, 2915 Atlantic Avenue, Atlantic City, NJ 08401; 609 FISH FUN; FAX 609 875-1095.

Norfolk Festevents

Norfolk Festevents coordinates all aspects of Norfolk's waterfront ship visits program. Facilities in Norfolk include the new, state-of-the-art Nauticus International Pier located at the National Maritime Center. Regular ship visits scheduled include tall ships and government vessels from the Navy, Coast Guard and the National Oceanographic and Atmospheric Administration (NOAA). The pier is immediately adjacent to Town Point Park, site of free weekly festivals, concerts and special events, and the Waterside Festival Marketplace, with 150 shops and restaurants open seven days a week. The Nauticus International Pier is centrally located and within short walking distance to downtown Norfolk shopping areas, a wide variety of restaurants and nightclubs, the YMCA, harbor and dinner cruise boats, churches, cultural activities such as theater and opera, the Chrysler Museum, and the MacArthur Memorial.

Karen Scherberger, Executive Director, Tim Jones, Ship Director, Norfolk Festevents, 120 West Main St., Norfolk, VA 23510; 804 441-2345; FAX 804 441-5198.

Northern S.T.A.R (Sail Training and Renewal)

The Northern S.T.A.R. programs focuses on maritime history and ecological marine biology, with particular emphasis on crew experience, expeditionary learning and early intervention.

Jack Ewing, Northern S.T.A.R., 04300 Sequanta Rd., Charlevoix, MI 49720; 616 547-9674.

Ocean Challenge

Ocean Challenge, Inc. (OCI), offers dynamic learning adventure called Class Afloat, which tracks 50 multinational high school students as they sail around the world aboard the 188' barkentine *Concordia*. At sea, Class Afloat students pursue a rigorous accredited academic program while learning to sail as crew members aboard *Concordia*. In port, they meet and in some cases live with indigenous people and learn about their culture.

Through the Class Afloat Education program, student on shore will experience the wonder and adventure of a 30,000-mile circumnavigation — crossing the Atlantic Ocean, Mediterranean Sea, Suez Canal, Red Sea, Indian Ocean and Pacific Ocean, and visiting 35 ports along the way.

A Class Afloat hands-on activities guide will feature the extraordinary multidisciplinary aspects of an ocean voyage: geography, world history, cultures, science of sailing, math, weather, marine wildlife, as well as planning, decision-making, discipline, confidence, teamwork and tolerance.

A two-page Class Afloat newsletter delivered by fax or by mail will link classrooms to the ongoing adventure. Each newsletter includes an article written by one of the students aboard *Concordia*, a Ship's Log, a Locator Map, a Class Afloat news sections, a Q & A, and an Extra Credit activity.

Rich Wilson, President, 20 Park Plaza, Suite 424, Boston, MA 02116; 617 357-0055.

Ocean Voyages

Ocean Voyages was founded seventeen years ago to provide participatory educational sailing programs throughout the world. Programs are open to sailing enthusiasts of all ages. Most programs run from one to four weeks in length. Ocean Voyages works with educators and institutions to design customized programs for youth participation.

Ocean Voyages works towards preserving the maritime heritage of the United States and providing opportunities for people to gain sailing education and seafaring experience. Coastal and inter-island programs are available in addition to offshore passage-making opportunities. Program areas include Hawaii, California, the Pacific Northwest, Galapagos Islands, Aegean Sea, Caribbean, French Polynesia and New Zealand, as well as Pacific and Atlantic Ocean crossings.

Mary T. Crowley, Director, Ocean Voyages, 1709 Bridgeway, Sausalito, CA 94965; 415 332-4681; FAX 415 332-7460.

Sail Baltimore

Sail Baltimore, a 501(c)(3) non-profit volunteer organization founded in 1975, is a community service organization located in Baltimore. Its primary mission is to offer maritime educational experiences to the general public, visitors, local citizens, children and disadvantaged youth, to stimulate the economy of the City of Baltimore and surrounding communities, to increase regional tourism, to provide a forum and network for encouraging business development opportunities in an international arena, and to foster international cultural exchange.

The board of directors of Sail Baltimore accomplishes its mission through recruiting, planning and hosting visits of various types of ships — tall, naval, non-naval vessels of historic interest and other vessels whose presence in the harbor offers an educational but non-commercial experience.

Sail Baltimore also produces special events designed to attract people to the city's waterfronts. Utilizing the skills of board, staff and volunteers, which include event marketing, management and publicity, Sail Baltimore has produced several successful tall ships events and water parades over the past ten years. We work in partnership with ASTA, the Baltimore Office of Promotion and area yacht clubs and corporations to produce these quality events.

Carmel Locey, Executive Director, Sail Baltimore, Suite B, 200 West Lombard St., Baltimore, MD 21201-2517; 410 752-8632; FAX 410 385-0361.

Sail Martha's Vineyard

Sail Martha's Vineyard is a non-profit organization dedicated to preserving the maritime heritage and culture of the island of Martha's Vineyard. Its activities are centered on encouraging island children to be comfortable on the water by offering beginning boat handling and sailing instruction free of charge, on facilitating maritime-related projects in the public schools, and on attracting interesting and historic vessels to the island. The organization depends entirely on volunteers, grants and private donations for its support.

Joseph B. Hall, President, Sail Martha's Vineyard, PO Box 1998, Sail Martha's Vineyard, Vineyard Haven, MA 02568; 508 696-7644.

Saint Croix Pilots

Captain Michael S. Phelps, St. Croix Yacht Club, Teague Bay, St. Croix, USVI 00820; 809 772-8315.

Saint John Port Corporation

Saint John, New Brunswick, is Canada's first incorporated city, incorporated by Royal Charter in 1785, On June 24, 1604, St. John the Baptist Day, French explorer Samuel de Champlain landed at the mouth of a mighty river on the Bay of Fundy. In honor of the day he proclaimed that the river and the harbor at its mouth be named St. John. The modern port is located near the head of the Bay of Fundy, which is famous for its extreme tides, the highest in the world. In addition, the Bay of Fundy is also home to 15 species of whale which thrive in the rich feeding grounds around the Fundy Isles in southwestern New Brunswick. These gentle giants are drawn to the Bay by the bountiful supply of plankton which blooms in the nutrient rich water churned up twice a day by the powerful tides.

With its dynamic complex of modern terminals, port facilities and services, and equipment, the Port of St. John makes an excellent stop for sailing ships. In addition to its maritime industries, the modern city enjoys boasts summer festivals, uptown boutiques, and a vibrant night life to delight sailors old and young.

Peter Clark, Saint John Port Corp., 133 Prince William St., PO Box 6429, Station A, Saint John, New Brunswick E2L 4R8 Canada; 506 636-4869; FAX 506 636-4443.

Salem Maritime
National Historic Site

Salem Maritime National Historic Site, administered by the National Park Service, U.S. Department of the Interior, was the country's first National Historic Site. Situated along the harbor in Salem, Massachusetts (20 miles northeast of Boston), it is the best remaining representative of early American maritime activities and their significant contributions to the founding and development of the United States.

The National Historic Site encompasses about 9.5 acres at the center of what was once the main waterfront section of the city. The principal resources include three reconstructed historic wharves – Derby, Hatch's and Central – extending into Salem Harbor and backed by rows of government, residential, and commercial structures, including the U. S. Custom House, elegant homes of the sea captains and merchants, and the more ordinary homes of craftsman.

Current reconstruction projects include: the 1797 three-masted East Indiaman merchant ship, *Friendship*, which will be berthed at Derby Wharf, and the new Central Wharf home of the Tall Ship Visiting Vessels program. Tall ships played an integral role in Salem's history and continue to do so at the Salem Maritime National Historic Site; they capture the imagination and transport visitors back to a time when harbors were filled with ships, wharves were lined with warehouses, and the waterfront buildings were bustling with activity. Visit the Salem Maritime National Historic Site and experience an appreciation of the significance of maritime enterprise on our national heritage.

Peter D. LaChapelle, Chief of Visitor Services, Salem Maritime National Historic Site, 174 Derby Street, Salem, MA 01970; 508 740-1680; FAX 508 740-1685.

Sausalito Tall Ships Society

The Sausalito Tall Ships Society (STSS) is a non-profit organization dedicated to educating people in traditional nautical skills and supporting the operation and preservation of vintage sailing vessels, particularly tall ships. The Society's goals include promoting the visit of tall ships to San Francisco Bay, providing shore-side education and shipboard learning experience for members, raising funds for cadet scholarships and collaborating with other maritime organizations.

The society raises funds or locates other sources of money for scholarships to enable teenagers to sail aboard tall ships. Each year, the organization helps to send cadets on California's state tall ship, the *Californian*, and occasionally on other vessels, including *Concordia* from Canada, and the *Kaisei* from Japan. The organization has helped provide free docking and shore support for the visits of the *Kaisei, Pride of Baltimore II, Pacific Swift, Lady Washington* and *Tole Mour*. In 1995, STSS planned and hosted the first ASTA meeting of 50 West Coast sail training ship operators, supporters and current and former ASTA board members in San Francisco. This year the society celebrated its 10th anniversary.

Alice C. Cochran, President, Sausalito Tall Ships Society, PO Box 926, Sausalito, CA 94966; 415 457-8997.

Sydney (Nova Scotia) Harbour Ports

Sydney Harbour Ports Board is a non-profit organization which promotes the Harbour of Sydney and activities within, including those at the three ports in Sydney Harbour: Sydney itself, Sydport and Marine Atlantic. Supplies are available at the three ports within Sydney Harbour, and the ports are only a 15-minute drive from the international airport.

George Wheeliker, Executive Director, Sydney Harbour Ports Regional Development Board, PO Box 248, North Sydney, Nova Scotia B2A 3M3 Canada; 902 564-4344.

Urban Harbors Institute

The Urban Harbors Institute conducts multidisciplinary research on urban harbor issues ranging from water quality to waterfront development. The Institute sponsors workshops, symposia and educational programs; it also publishes reports and proceedings, provides technical assistance to community and business leaders and the general public and maintains a resource library. Annually, the institute sponsors an expedition for six geography credits, aboard the schooner *Sylvina W. Beal* and day programs are offered aboard various schooners from the New England region.

The Institute is associated with the University of Massachusetts' programs in environmental sciences, geography, and management. Its core staff, senior associates, and researchers have expertise in public policy, coastal resource management, marine law, economics, waterfront planning, international coastal zone management and education.

Madeleine Walsh, Urban Harbors Institute, University of Massachusetts, 100 Morrissey Blvd., Boston, MA 02125; 617 287-5570; FAX 617 287-5575.

U.S. Merchant Marine Academy

Sail, Power and Crew Squadron, U.S. Merchant Marine Academy, Kings Point, NY 11024-1699; 516 773-5396.

Vane Brothers
Marine Safety and Services, Inc.

Bob Alexander, General Manager, 4565 Progress Road, Suite 2B, Norfolk, VA 23502; 804 858-2501.

Venus de Milo

Monte C. Feris, Venus de Milo, 75 Grand Army Highway, Swansea, MA 02777-3296; 508 678-3901.

Williams College-Mystic Seaport Maritime Studies Program

Williams College-Mystic Maritime Studies Program offers undergraduates the opportunity to focus a semester on the study of the sea. Students take four William College courses at Mystic Seaport: maritime history, literature of the sea, marine science (either oceanography or marine ecology), and marine policy. Academic are enhanced by hands-on training aboard Mystic Seaport's many ships, as well as by maritime skills classes in sailing, wood carving, sea music and climbing aloft on a square rigger.

Three field seminars are incorporated into the curriculum each semester. The fall semester voyages offshore for nearly two weeks in the North Atlantic and the spring semester to southern waters, both aboard a 130-foot staysail schooner. This expedition involves intensive student participation in sailing the vessel. In addition to the excitement of spending days out of sight of land, students also travel to Nantucket and the Port of New York for the Atlantic Coast Field Seminar, and out west to California and Oregon, for the newly introduced Pacific Coast Field Seminar.

Student return to Mystic and apply knowledge gained in their field experiences toward their research projects in history, marine science and marine policy. A full semester of credit is granted through Williams College. Financial aid is available.

Anna Fitzgerald, Assistant Director of Admissions, Williams College-Mystic Seaport Maritime Studies Program, Mystic Seaport Museum, 75 Greenmanville Ave., PO Box 6000, Mystic, CT 06355-0990; 203 572-5359; FAX 203 572-5329. E-mail: Williams@Mystic.org.

Wooden Boat Foundation

The Wooden Boat Foundation is a non-profit organization located in Port Townsend, Washington, committed to fostering respect for self, community and environment by providing a center for unique educational experiences through the exploration of traditional maritime skills. Located in Washington's "Victorian Seaport," the Foundation offers its members and community a comprehensive maritime library, a chart room for classes and seminars, a woodworking shop, and a public retail store featuring maritime books and gifts. Our educational programs are the Summer Sea Symposium, small boat summer sailing for students and adults, 1- to 12-day programs and the Annual Wooden Boat Festival, now in its 20th year. With 14,000 visitors, the festival features workshops, seminars, demonstrations, classic boat regattas, music, Native American canoes and culture, model oat building and fish prints for children. Proceeds from the event enable the Foundation to develop and support its educational mission.

David King, Planning Director, Cupola House, #2 Point Hudson, Port Townsend, WA 98368; 360 385-3628.

WoodenBoat School

The WoodenBoat School is located on a 64-acre waterfront campus in Brooklin, Maine. Founded 14 years ago, the school's twin focus is on wooden boat building and sailing instruction taught by experienced sailors in cutters, friendship sloops, ketches and more than 20 assorted small craft ranging from a 7'6" Nutshell sailing pram to a 23' Cyclone trimaran. A majority of the course offerings, which last no more than two weeks, teach various aspects of boat building and woodworking. Instruction in related crafts such as sail making, marine surveying, marine mechanics and electronics, rigging/handwork, and painting and varnishing is also offered.

Rich Hilsinger, Director, WoodenBoat School, PO Box 78, Naskeag Rd., Brooklin, ME 04616; 207 359-4651; FAX 207 359 8920.

Youth Adventure

Ernestine Bennett, PO Box 23 Mercer Island, WA 98040; 206 232-4024; FAX 206 232-4024.

International Sail Training Associations

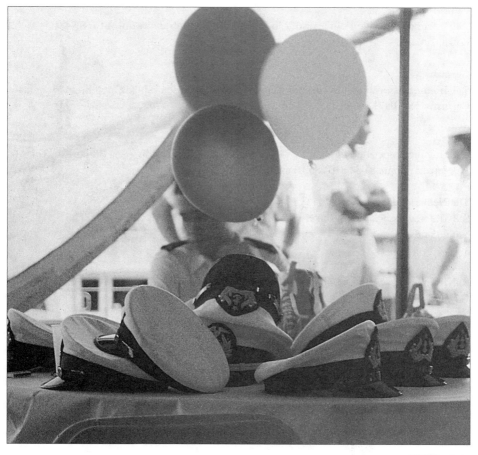

ASTA file photo

There are hundreds of sail training programs around the world. The following organizations have functions corresponding to those of the American Sail Training Association and will be able to supply information about the sail training opportunities in their respective countries.

Australia
Sail Training Association of Western Australia, PO Boc 1100, Freemantle 6160, Western Australia; Phone: 09 430 4105, Fax: 09 430 4494.

Canada
Sail Training Association of Canada, Box 709, Station B, Ottawa, Ontario, K1P 5P8, Canada; Phone: 705-728-8265.

Finland
Sail Training Association of Finland, c/o Kotkan Satamalaitos, Laivurinkatu 7, SF-48100 Kotka, Finland.

Germany
Sail Training Association of Germany, Hafenhaus, Columbusbahnhof, 27568 Bremerhaven, Germany; Fax: 0471 94588-45.

Japan
Sail Training Association of Japan, 1-14-4 Hongo, Nanyo-Do, Building. 2F, Bunkyo-ku, Tokyo 113, Japan; Phone: 81-3-3818-2852, Fax: 81-3-3816-1673.

The Netherlands
Sail Training Association of the Netherlands, Postbus 55, 2340 AB Oegstgeest, The Netherlands.

Poland
Sail Training Association of Poland, Gdynska Fundacja Zeglarska, al Zjednocczenia, 3, 81-963, Gdynia 1, Poland.

Portugal
APORVELA, Centro de Operacoes, Doca do Terreiro doTrigo, 1100 Lisboa, Portugal; Phone: 351-1-887-68-54, Fax: 351-1-887 38 85.

Russia
Sail Training Association of Russia, St. Petersburg Engineering Marine College, 15A Kosaya Lina, St. Petersburg, 199026, Russia.

United Kingdom
International Sail Training Association, 5 Mumby Road, Gosport, Hants PO12 1AA, UK; Phone: 44 1705 586 367, Fax: 44 1705 584 661.

Sail Tall Ships!

Membership in the American Sail Training Association is open to all individuals and organizations with an interest in the whole spectrum of sea experience – from pure adventure to academic pursuit. ASTA membership keeps you informed and linked to the tall ships of North America and Canada and sail training around the world.

We "get the word out" about sail training programs and tall ship events, activities and educational opportunities – ASTA brings people and ships together. ASTA is a bridge to the future, building on traditions from ships, sailing, and the sea.

Roger Archibald photo

ASTA

Billet Bank Registration

PERSONAL:

Last Name _____ First Name _____ M.I.

Permanent Address _____ Apt. No. _____

City _____ State _____ Zip Code _____ Country _____

Temporary Address _____ Apt. No. _____

_____ Valid Thru Date _____

City _____ State _____ Zip Code _____ Country _____

Permanent Phone No. _____ Current Phone No. _____ Valid Thru Date _____

DOCUMENTATION:

Marine License:
Rating(s) _____ Issue No. _____ Date of Renewal _____

Radar Endorsement: ☐ Limited / ☐ Unlimited?   United States Merchant Mariners Document? ☐ Yes / ☐ No
Renewal Date _____   Rating(s) _____

Auxiliary Sail Endorsement?   Towing Endorsement?   FCC Marine Radio Operator's License?
   ☐ Yes / ☐ No   ☐ Yes / ☐ No   ☐ Yes / ☐ No

High School Attended_____ Diploma? ☐ Yes / ☐ No

College Attended _____

Degree? ☐ Yes / ☐ No   Major _____ Minor _____

Other Related Education _____

MARINE EXPERIENCE:

Sailed On: (Check all that apply)
☐ Schooner ☐ Square Rigger ☐ Ketch ☐ Yawl ☐ Power Yacht ☐ Tug ☐ Launch Other _____

Vessel Size: (Please indicate exact LOA of vessels served on) 400' +_____ 300' +_____ 250' +_____

200' +_____ 150' +_____ 100' +_____ 50' +_____ 25' +_____ Other_____

Vessel Tonnage: ☐ 1000 GT ☐ 500 GT ☐ 300 GT ☐ 250 GT ☐ 200 GT
(Check all that apply) ☐ 150 GT ☐ 100 GT ☐ 50 GT ☐ 25 GT

Vessel Certifications: (Check all that apply)
☐ USCG ☐ ABS ☐ SOLAS ☐ T ☐ K ☐ H ☐ SSV ☐ 6 Pak ☐ Uncertified Vessels ☐ Foreign Registry

Firefighting Certificate? ☐ Yes / ☐ No   Medical Courses (Rating)_____

U.S. Passport No. _____ International Shot Card_____

SEATIME:

Approx. Total Seatime: _____ (In Days)   Approx. Total Sailtime: _____(In Days)

Last Vessel Served On _____

Industry Reference(s) _____

_____

Please indicate your specific interests:

Volunteer Work_____ Crew Position: Licensed_____ / Unlicensed_____ Cook_____ Deckhand_____

Engineer_____ Educator_____ Mate_____ Captain_____ Office Administration_____

Additional Info:

_____
_____
_____

Office Use Only

Date Received_____ Date Entered_____ Computer Directory_____ Entry #_____

Membership in the American Sail Training Association is open to all individuals and organizations with an interest in the whole spectrum of sea experience -- from pure adventure to academic pursuit. ASTA membership keeps you informed and linked to the tall ships of North America and sail training around the world.

We "get the word out" about sail training programs and tall ships events, activities and educational opportunities -- ASTA brings people and ships together. ASTA is a bridge to the future, building on traditions from ships, sailing and the sea.

Opportunities for Membership in ASTA

Individual $45 (Tax-deductible value - $15)

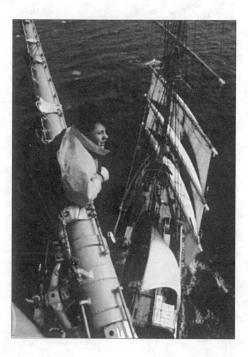

❏ Complimentary copy of the annual *Directory of Tall Ships and Sail Training*

❏ Subscription to *Running Free*, the ASTA newsletter, to keep you up to date on tall ship news, events and job opportunities

❏ Member's discounts for one person at all ASTA programs, such as ASTA's annual Sail Training Conference, Safety Under Sail Seminars and the International Safety Forum

❏ Resume´/Credentials listing in ASTA Billet Bank

Junior $30 (Tax deductible value - $0)

❏ Open to sailors 22 years of age and younger

❏ All of the benefits of Individual membership above

Family $75 (Tax deductible value - $35)

❏ Open to two members at the same address

❏ All of the benefits of Individual Membership above *plus:*

❏ Two ASTA coffee mugs

❏ Member discounts applicable to two

Supporting $250 (Tax deductible value - $215)

Organizations, ports, companies and associates of tall ships

❏ All of the benefits of Individual Membership above *plus:*

❏ Listing on the Sponsorship Page in the ASTA *Directory of Tall Ships and Sail Training*

❏ Listing in *Running Free,* the ASTA Newsletter

❏ Set of four ASTA Coffee Mugs

Corporate or Patron
$1,000 (Tax deductible value - $900)

For businesses or individuals wishing to express a greater commitment to ASTA's goals

❏ All of the benefits of Supporting Membership above *plus:*

❏ Two complimentary tickets to the ASTA Annual Awards Dinner

❏ Choice of ASTA Tall Ships Necktie *or* Blazer Patch

Sail Training Organizations (see below)
(Tax deductible value- $0)

Organizations operating sail training vessels or tall ships are enrolled for the Calendar Year- renewable between January and May of that year

❏ Full-page listing (including photo of your vessel) in ASTA *Directory of Tall Ships and Sail Training*

❏ 10 complimentary copies of the *Directory*

❏ Subscription to *Running Free,* the ASTA newsletter, and editorial opportunities

❏ Notice of available crew registered with the ASTA Billet Bank

❏ Access to the ASTA Marine Insurance Program

❏ Publication of your ship's news/job opportunities in *Running Free*

❏ Member's discounts for all staff to ASTA Programs: Annual Sail Training Conference, Safety Under Sail Seminars and the International Safety Forum.

Affiliate $100 *(Tax deductible value-$0)*

Open to non-profit organizations which do not operate vessels but do offer sail training or sea education programs (Scouts, schools, colleges, etc.)

❏   Listing in the Program section of the ASTA *Directory of Tall Ships and Sail Training*

❏   10 complimentary copies of the *Directory*

❏   Subscription to *Running Free*, the ASTA Newsletter

❏   Discounts for Affiliate Member staff representatives to attend the ASTA Sail Training Conference, Safety Under Sail Seminars and the International Safety Forum

American Sail Training Association

47 Bowen's Wharf, P.O. Box 1459
Newport, Rhode Island   02840
(401) 846-1775   Fax: (401) 849-5400

Sail training is adventure travel ...

Thousands of sailing ships -- tall and small -- offer adventure travel under sail throughout the world. ASTA member vessels provide blue water adventure, coastal vacations, corporate team building and education at sea -- from dockside history programs to underway classroom field trips to on-board college semesters.

The American Sail Training Association supports and promotes sail training and sea education in North America, providing people of all ages, backgrounds and abilities access to the adventure of a lifetime.

Sail training is more than learning *to* sail. On a tall ship you learn *from* sailing -- from the ship, from the sea, from yourself.

Get underway to expand your horizons...

Join ASTA today!

Yes, I/we want to join the American Sail Training Association!

Name _____

Organization _____

Mailing Address _____

City _____ State _____ Zip _____

Country _____ Phone Number _____

Fax Number _____ E-mail _____

Please enroll me/us in the following membership category:

Associate Memberships
_____ Individual $45   _____ Supporting $250
_____ Junior $30   _____ Corporate $1,000
_____ Family $75

Professional Trade Memberships
_____ Affiliate (youth groups and schools) $100
_____ Sail Training Organization (membership fee based on annual budget)
                    _____ less than $250,000 $175
                    _____ between $250,000 and $500,000 $225
                    _____ greater than $500,000 $275

Associate memberships are renewable on date of anniversary.
Professional trade memberships are for calendar year.
Address in Canada/Mexico please add US $12 to cover additional postage and handling.
Membership outside North America please add US $16.

Check Enclosed (US Bank Only) _____   Visa _____   MasterCard _____

Card Number _____ Exp. _____

Name on Card _____

Winners! First Place in ASTA's First-Ever Official Annual Professional Tall Ship Crew Rowing Regatta — Pride of Baltimore II.

ASTA File photo

The Ship's Store

Sail Tall Ships! A Directory of Sail Training and Adventure at Sea	*$15.00*
Guidelines for Educational Programs Under Sail	*$14.00*
1995 International Safety Forum Proceedings	*$25.00*
American Photographers at the Turn of the Century: Travel & Trekking	*$22.95*

Collection of beautifully reproduced photo essays on world travel, includes Roger Archibald's photos and writings on his experiences aboard ASTA member vessels. Purchase of this book includes an automatic donation of $5.00 to ASTA

The Sailing Experience - VHS format, 9 min.	*$18.00*
ASTA Ceramic Coffee Mug	*$6.00*
Tall Ships 2000® Ceramic Coffee Mug	*$6.00*

ASTA Flags - Blue field with ASTA logo and letters, nylon with tape/grommets
Suitable for flying from your ship, home, or office

12" x 18"	*$15.00*
2' x 3'	*$20.00*
3' x 5'	*$25.00*
4' x 6'	*$30.00*
5' x 8'	*$40.00*

ASTA Pin - Logo in oval, pin back, pewter/copper finish	*$6.00*
ASTA Tie - Navy blue with white woven ASTA logo	*$25.00*
ASTA Blazer Patch	*$33.00*
Tall Ships 2000® T-Shirt	*$16.00*
Annalee Mobilitee Dolls Tall Ships® Sailor Duck	*$25.50*

All prices include shipping and handling. Payment may be made with US bank check, Visa or MasterCard.

Mail order information to: ASTA , 47 Bowen's Wharf, PO Box 1459, Newport, RI 02840 or call the ASTA office: (401) 846-1775

INDEX

Geographical Index
of ASTA Member Vessels

Clockwise from the Great Lakes

Great Lakes, Canada
Penetanguishene, Ont. (44°47'N, 79°56'W) *Bee, Tecumseth*
Kingston, Ont. (44°14'N, 76°30'W) *Fair Jeanne, St. Lawrence II*
Toronto, Ont. (43°42'N, 79°25'W) *Challenge*
Ottawa, Ont. (45°25'N, 75°43'W) *Black Jack*

Great Lakes, U.S.
Chicago, Ill. (41°53'N, 87°36'W) *Windy*
Suttons Bay, Mich. (44°58'N, 85°38'W) *Inland Seas*
Traverse City, Mich. (44°46'N, 85°38'W) *Madeline, Malabar, Welcome*
Northport, Mich. (45°09'N, 85°38'W) *Manitou*
Erie, Pa. (42°07'N, 80°05'W) *Niagara*
Kendall, N.Y. (43°20'N, 78°03'W) *Pilgrim*
Oswego, N.Y. (43°27'N, 76°31'W) *OMF Ontario*
Buffalo, N.Y. 42°52'N, 78°55'W) *Sea Lion*

Canadian Maritimes
Halifax, N.S. (44°40N, 63°35'W) *Dorothea*
Lunenburg, Nova Scotia (44°22'N, 64°19'W) *Bluenose II*

New England
Bar Harbor, Me. (44°24'N, 68°12'W) *Anawan, Francis Todd, Natalie Todd, Young America*
Castine, Me. (44°23'N. 68°48'W) *Bowdoin*
Rockland, Me. (44°06'N, 69°06'W) *Nathaniel Bowditch, Victory Chimes*
Camden, Me. (44°12'N, 69°03'W) *Angelique, Appledore II, Mary Day*
Bath, Me. (43°55'N, 69°49'W) *Chance, Maine*
Portland, Me. (43°40'N, 70°15'W) *Ocean Star, Palawan*
Gloucester, Mass. (42°36'N, 70°40'W) *Adventure, Ebb Tide*
Charlestown, Mass. (42°22'N, 71°03'W) USS *Constitution*
Boston, Mass. (42°21'N, 71°03'W) *Harvey Gamage, Liberty, Liberty Clipper, Spirit of Massachusetts*
Orleans, Mass. (41°47'N, 69°58'W) *Picara*
Woods Hole, Mass. (41°32'N, 70°40'W) *Corwith Cramer, Westward*
Martha's Vineyard, Mass. (41°27'N, 70°36'W) *Shenandoah*
Fall River, Mass. (41°44'N, 71°08'W) *Bounty*
Marion, Mass. (41°42'N, 70°46'W) *Tabor Boy*
New Bedford, Mass. (41°38'N, 70°55'W) *Ernestina*
Newport, R.I. (41°30'N, 71°20'W) *Adirondack, Coronet, Endeavour, Geronimo, Gleam, Isabelle, Land's End, Northern Light, Providence*
Mystic, Conn. (41°21'N, 71°58'W) *Brilliant, Joseph Conrad, Mystic Whaler, Sylvina Beal*

New London, Conn. (41°22'N, 72°06'W) USCG *Eagle*
New Haven, Conn. (41°18'N, 72°55'W) *Quinnipiack*
Bridgeport, Conn. (41°10'N, 73°11'W) *Black Pearl, John E. Pfriem,* "HMS" *Rose*
Stamford, Conn. (41°02'N, 73°33'W) *Soundwaters*
Greenwich, Conn. (41°01'N, 73°37'W) *Alert*

Midatlantic
Poughkeepsie, N.Y. (41°47'N, 73°57'W) *Clearwater*
Croton-on-Hudson, N.Y. (41°11'N, 73°52'W) *Halve Maen*
New York City (40°42'N, 74°00') *Lettie G. Howard, Pioneer*
Atlantic City, N.J. (39°21'N, 74°25'W) *Young America*
Cape May, N.J. (38°55'N, 74°56'W) *Yankee*
Bivalve, N.J. (39°13'N, 75°02'W) *A. J. Meerwald*
Philadelphia, Pa. (39°57'N, 75°08'W) *Bill of Rights, Gazela of Philadelphia, Moshulu, New Way*
Wilmington, Del. (39°43'N, 75°31'W) *Lisa, Norseman*
Baltimore, Md. (39°16'N, 76°35'W) *Clipper City, Lady Maryland, Minnie V., Pride of Baltimore II*
Alexandria, Va. (38°48'N, 77°02'W) *Alexandria, Federalist*
Cobb Island, Md. (38°14'N, 76°49'W) *Harold K. Acker, Mabel Stevens*
Oakley, Md. (38°16'N, 76°44'W) *Fyrdraca, Gyrfalcon*
Jamestown, Va. (37°12'N, 76°47'W) *Susan Constant*
Norfolk, Va. (36°51'N, 76°18'W) *American Rover, Norfolk Rebel*
Manteo, N.C. (35°54'N, 75°40'W) *Elizabeth II*

Southeast & Caribbean
Fort Lauderdale, Fla. (26°07'N, 80°07'W) *Adirondack, Compass Rose*
Miami, Fla. (25°46'N, 80°08'W) *Heritage of Miami II, William H. Albury*
Key West, Fla. (24°33'N, 81°48'W) *Liberty, Misty Isles, Odyssey*
Tortola, British Virgin Is. (18°23'N, 64°42'W) *Ocean Adventure, Picton Castle*

Gulf Coast
St. Petersburg, Fla. (27°46'N, 82°37'W) *Bounty*
Apalachicola, Fla. (29°43'N, 84°59'W) *Governor Stone*
Biloxi, Miss. (30°24'N, 88°51'W) *Glenn L. Swetman, Mike Sekul*
Galveston, Tex. (29°18'N, 94°48'W) *Elissa*
Corpus Christi, Tex. (27°48'N, 97°23'W) *Niña*

California
San Diego, Calif. (32°43'N, 117°10'W) *Odyssey, Star of India*
Newport Beach, Calif. (33°36'N, 117°53'W) *Alaska Eagle, Argus*
Los Angeles, Calif. (33°43'N, 118°16'W) *Swift of Ipswich*
Dana Point, Calif. (33°45'N, 118°12'W) *Californian, Pigrim, Virginia*
San Francisco, Calif. (37°48'N, 122°28') *Alma*
Sausalito, Calif. (37°51N, 122°29'W) *Dariabar, Hawaiian Chieftain, Maramel*
Richmond, Calif. (37°55'N, 122°22'W) *Nehemiah*

Pacific Northwest
Gray's Harbor, Wash. (46°55'N, 124°08'W) *Lady Washington*
Friday Harbor, Wash. (48°32'N, 123°W) *Mahina Tiare*
Anacortes, Wash. (48°31'N, 122°37'W) *Discovery*
Port Townsend, Wash. (48°07'N, 122°45'W) *Adventuress*

Seattle, Wash. (47°36'N, 122°20'W) *Martha, Zodiac*
Victoria, B.C. (48°26'N, 123°23'W) *Pacific Swift, Robertson*

Pacific & Indian Oceans
Honolulu, Hawaii (21°18'N, 157°52'W) *Tole Mour*
Auckland, New Zealand (36°50'S, 174°47'W) *Mahina Tiare*
Fremantle, Australia (32°03'S, 115°45'E) *Sovereign of the Seas*

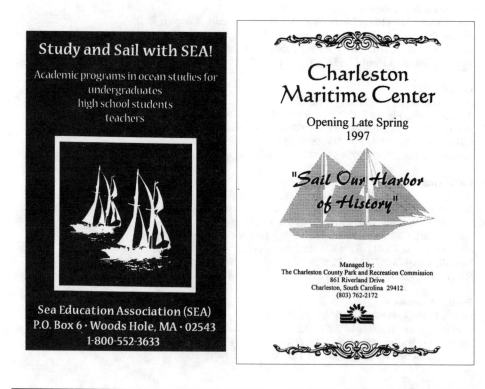

Index

Abaco, Bahamas schools, 171
Abeking & Rasmussen, 97, 170
Aberdeen (Wash.) Public Development
    Authority, 112
Acadia National Park, 94, 131
Achaios, 88
Aconcagua Foundation, 85
ActionQuest/ActionSail, 186
Adams, John Quincy, 178
Adirondack, 55
Adventure, 56
Adventuress, 57
A. J. Meerwald, 54
Alaska Eagle, 58
Albatross, 45
Albury, William H., 171
Alden, John, 83
Alden, Michael, 114
Alert, 59
Alexander Hall and Sons Yard, 88
Alexander, Bob, 196
Alexandria Seaport Foundation, 60, 93
Alexandria, 60
Alk, 45
Allard, Michael F., 146
Allen, Charlie, 67
Alma, 61
America's Cup, 90, 98, 139
America, 62
American Rover, 63
American Sail Training Association, 25, 27,
    49, 70, 103; Billet Bank Registration, 202-
    203; History, 17-18; Membership infor-
    mation, 201; Programs and Professional
    Services, 20; Rallies, 18; 'Running Free,'
    21; Sail Training Program of the Year,
    134; Ship's Store, 208; Tall Ships 2000®,
    24-27
Amistad Project, 178
Anawan, 179
Ancient Mysteries: Vikings in North America, 138
AndaVela, 186
Angelique, 64
Annalee Mobilitee Dolls, 172
Apalachicola Maritime Museum, Inc., 100
Apex Predator Investigation, 97
APORVELA, 200
Applecraft, Inc., 138
Appledore II, 65

Aquaculture Foundation, 70, 109
Argus, 66
Arnold, Edward, 159
Artisans College, 186-87
Ashronia Christian Cadet & Mission Ship
    Association, 183
Association for Great Lakes History, 119, 168
ASTACE, 170
Atlantic Challenge, 187
Attraction Vessels, 34
Australia, 183, 200; Australian Bicentenary
    Tall Ships, 17 ; Sail Training Association
    of, 200

Bagley, Chris, 67, 164
Bailey, Howdy, 106, 137
Baker, William A., 89, 155
Baltimore clipper, 116, 150
Baltimore, City of, 193
Banks, Bruce, 190
Barcelona Maritime Museum, 136
Barney, Joshua, 93
Barney, Tara, 188
Bartlett, Bob, 91
Bay Area Convention and Visitors Bureau,
    187-88
Beal, Charles Henry, 162
Beaufort Mariners Museum, 101
Beck, Michael, 81
Becuna, 189
Bee, 67, 164
Bennett, Ernestine, 198
Benton, Nick, 102
Bermuda Race, 113, 167
Bettencourt, Emmanuel, 186
Billet Bank, 20-21; Registration, 202-203
Bill of Rights, 49, 68
Biloxi Schooner Project, 99, 127
'Biography: Leif Ericson,' 138
Black Jack, 69
Black Pearl, 70
Blades, Hugh, 153
Blocher, William L., 79
Blohm & Voss, 86
Blonder, Fred, 95, 101
Blount Marine Corp., 116
Bluenose II Preservation Trust, 71
Bluenose II, 71
BOAT/U.S. Foundation for Boating Safety,
    188

Vessels by Classification

Attraction vessels
Bounty, Gazela of Philadelphia, Halve Maen,
"HMS" Rose, Niagara, Sea Lion, Star of India,
Welcome.

Freight and miscellaneous (Subchapter I)
Tole Mour.

Ocean Research Vessel (Subchapter U)
Dariabar, John E. Pfriem.

Passenger Vessel (Subchapter T)
A. J. Meerwald, Adirondack, Adventuress, Alert,
America, Amercan Rover, Angelique, Appledore
II, Argus, Bill of Rights, Bowdoin, Brilliant,
Californian, Clearwater, Elissa, Ernestina,
Francis Todd, Gleam, Glenn L. Swetman,
Governor Stone, Harvey Gamage, Hawaiian
Chieftain, Inland Seas, Lady Maryland, Lady
Washington, Liberty, Liberty Clipper, Malabar,
Manitou, Mary Day, Minnie V., Mystic Whaler,
Natalie Todd, Nathaniel Bowditch, Nehemiah,
New Way, Northern Light, OMF Ontario,
Palawan, Pioneer, Pride of Baltimore II,

Providence, Quinnipiack, Shenandoah,
Soundwaters, Spirit of Massachusetts, Swift of
Ipswich, Sylvina Beal, Victory Chimes, William
H. Albury, Windy, Yankee, Young America,
Zodiac.

Sailing school vessel (Subchapter R)
"HMS" Rose, Alaska Eagle, Bowdoin, Brilliant,
Corwith Cramer, Discovery, Ernestina,
Geronimo, Lettie G. Howard, Niña, Spirit of
Massachusetts, Tabor Boy, Tole Mour, Virginia,
William H. Albury.

Uninspected yachts
Bounty, Gazela of Philadelphia, Gyrfalcon,
Harold K. Acker, Land's End, Lisa, Mabel
Stevens, Madeline, Niagara, Picara, Pilgrim,
Pilgrim, Virginia.

Canadian passenger vessel
Challenge (Minor Waters II), Pacific Swift,
Robertson.

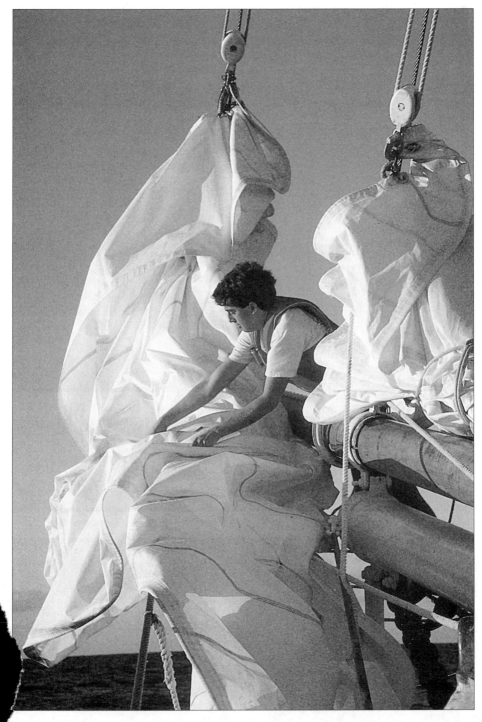

Roger Archibald photo